All Pretty HORSES NOTES

including
- *Life and Background of the Author*
- *Introduction to the Novel*
- *A Brief Synopsis*
- *List of Characters*
- *Critical Commentaries*
- *Critical Essay*
- *Character Web*
- *Map*
- *Review Questions and Essay Topics*
- *Selected Bibliography*

By Jeanne Inness, Ph.D.

INCORPORATED
LINCOLN, NEBRASKA 68501

Project Editor

Elizabeth Netedu Kuball

Acquisitions Editor

Greg Tubach

ISBN 0-7645-8551-7
© Copyright 1993
by
Cliffs Notes, Inc.
All Rights Reserved
Printed in U.S.A.

2000 Printing

The Cliffs Notes logo, the names "Cliffs" and Cliffs Notes," and the black and yellow diagonal-stripe cover design are all registered trademarks belonging to Cliffs Notes, Inc., and may not be used in whole or in part without written permission.

Cliffs Notes, Inc.   Lincoln, Nebraska

CONTENTS

Life and Background of the Author 5

Introduction to the Novel 6

A Brief Synopsis 12

List of Characters 15

Critical Commentaries 18
    Chapter I 18
    Chapter II 29
    Chapter III 48
    Chapter IV 55

Critical Essay 66
    The Horses of All the Pretty Horses
    and the American Dream 66

Review Questions and Essay Topics 72

Selected Bibliography 74

McCarthy's Major Works 74

**Critical Works about McCarthy
and the Southwest** 74

ALL THE PRETTY HORSES
Notes

LIFE AND BACKGROUND OF THE AUTHOR

Cormac McCarthy was born Charles McCarthy (Cormac is the Gaelic version of Charles) on July 20, 1933, in Providence, Rhode Island. In 1937, the family moved to Knoxville, Tennessee, where his father, Charles Joseph McCarthy, was on the legal staff of the Tennessee Valley Authority. The third of six children, Cormac attended Catholic High School in Knoxville and entered the University of Tennessee in 1951 as a liberal arts major. In 1953, he joined the United States Air Force and served four years, spending part of that time in Alaska. He married Lee Holleman, with whom he had a son. Cormac and Lee divorced, and he married Anne de Lisle, with whom he had no children and from whom he also was divorced. He married a third time, to Jennifer Winkler, in 1998, and reportedly lives with her and their child in El Paso, Texas (McCarthy is reclusive and information on him is often difficult to confirm).

McCarthy has received numerous writing awards, including the William Faulkner Foundation award in 1965 for *The Orchard Keeper*, a Rockefeller Foundation grant, a Guggenheim fellowship, a MacArthur Foundation Grant, and the National Book Award in 1992 for *All the Pretty Horses*.

His published works include eight novels — *The Orchard Keeper, Outer Dark, Child of God, Suttree, Blood Meridian, All the Pretty Horses, The Crossing,* and *Cities of the Plain* — all published by Random House; a play in five acts called *The Stonemason*; and a screenplay called *The Gardener's Son*.

Although McCarthy guards his privacy and is not known to seek publicity, the University of Texas at El Paso has a Cormac McCarthy Society, which sponsors papers for literary conferences and holds gatherings where McCarthy's work is read and discussed. The society has a Web site at www.cormacmccarthy.com, which you can visit for more information. Scholarly attention to McCarthy has grown in the last decade, largely as a result of *All the Pretty Horses*, which brought him critical acclaim as well as popular appeal.

INTRODUCTION TO THE NOVEL

Set in west Texas and northern central Mexico in 1949, *All the Pretty Horses* is subtitled "Volume One, The Border Trilogy," indicating that it is the first of three books in a series. The tale is about two young men, John Grady Cole and Lacey Rawlins, who run away from their hometown on their horses and ride across Texas and northeastern Mexico. They start near San Angelo, Texas, and travel approximately 130 miles to near Langtry, Texas, where they cross the Rio Grande River into Mexico. From there, they ride approximately 180 miles farther, to a well-situated hacienda, where they land jobs as cowboys. John Grady is identified by his mother as "only sixteen," and we can assume that his good friend, Rawlins, is a similar age. Both boys are mature for their age and successfully negotiate their adventure south.

Structurally, *All the Pretty Horses* is quite simple. The story begins with the wake of John Grady Cole's grandfather and takes us through the two friends' adventures, from beginning to end, when they return to the San Angelo area from Mexico. In addition to telling the story of the boys' adventure, McCarthy introduces a love story between John Grady and Alejandra, reminiscent of William Shakespeare's *Romeo and Juliet*.

All the Pretty Horses is perhaps the most readable of McCarthy's work. But the book's accessibility should not lull the reader into thinking that this is a simple novel. To the contrary, the first 30 pages may require two readings in order for the reader to get into the story. McCarthy's technique of introducing characters only as "he" or "she" and not naming them for several pages, if ever, can make the story difficult to follow and warns us not to assume that the characters are easy to understand. In the first mention of a character, we see the surface skin and perhaps a description or action; later, we learn the character's name; and finally, the story unfolds. For example, we don't learn John Grady's name until the fifth page of the book. But it is the events of the entire book that fill in his character, and, even then, we must wait for the third book of the trilogy to get the complete picture of who John Grady is.

In the rich story of *All the Pretty Horses*, the variety of themes adds complexity and allows room for multiple interpretations. Loss of innocence and loss of the past are two parallel themes in the novel. The journey, or quest, theme is very important to the book (Cervantes' *Don Quixote*, another story about a horseback journey of two men, is the only work of literature mentioned in the novel). After embarking on this journey, John Grady and Rawlins are no longer children. Similarly, with the passing of John Grady's grandfather, the old West is also now lost.

Family relationships are another important motif in the novel. We learn of John Grady's family and how they affect him and his future. John Grady's mother left him in the care of the Mexican women when he was a baby and remained away from the ranch for a long period of time in his childhood. His father was away because of World War II, and, except for teaching him about horses, his relationship with his grandfather did not give him the nurturing he needed. Rawlins comes from a poorer family that he wants to escape, while Blevins, who is only about 13 years old, seems to have been on his own for a long time and has no family at all. All three of these boys (or young men, as they mature in the story) have suffered abandonment, psychologically and emotionally, if not actually. So they run away, to find fulfillment in the big world they imagine is waiting for them. Differing from these American families is the family history of the Rochas at La Purisima. The Rochas have lived with privilege. All have received excellent educational experiences and only suffer, if at all, from too much family interference, yet, the Rocha family has been molded by Spanish and European traditions as well as the Mexican Revolution. The aunt was educated in Europe, and Senor Rocha is well-read and knowledgeable about Spanish and European history. However, the Mexican Revolution, of 40 years earlier, has altered the hopes and dreams of family members. It has made the aunt cynical and controlling, Senor Rocha passive and withdrawn into his hobbies. This atmosphere makes Alejandra alienated from her family and adds to her attraction to John Grady, who is full of dreams and is a man of action and idealism. He seems like a hero, something the Rocha family has not known since the Mexican Revolution.

The jail scenes bring up the terrors of cruelty and the dark side of humans and can be compared to similar incarcerations in other great works of literature. Dostoevsky wrote about his own imprisonment in a classic memoir. Camus writes tellingly of jail in *The Stranger*, as does Sartre in "The Wall." James Jones' *From Here to Eternity* has a famous "in the brig" section, which details how to survive extreme incarceration. *Native Son* by Richard Wright is the famous novel of a young African American man caught and imprisoned.

Last, and most important, is the nature theme and the relationship between human beings and the earth. The horses play a central role in defining what McCarthy is saying about human existence. The horses may be eternal, just as Yeats' swans in "The Wild Swans at Coole," which return every year. Human life, especially human achievement, is transitory, ever changing. Nature survives and continues. Striving human beings, in contrast to Native Americans, for example, who accept the natural pattern of existence, are left to struggle, always hoping, but often left with only a sense of loss. Thus, the struggle, the adventure, the process is the only meaning for humans, because the successes, the material acquisitions are not permanent. John Grady's attempts to get a life on a ranch or hacienda are doomed. But his relationship to horses, representing the earth and nature, is fulfilled. We last see him riding his horse, part of the landscape.

Influences on McCarthy's work. The boys' journey is filled with camping scenes reminiscent of Ernest Hemingway's early Nick Adams tales, in which the joy of sleeping under the stars and drinking coffee around the campfire brings peace of mind and renewal. Other authors also influence McCarthy's work. In particular, scholars have noted the great influence of William Faulkner in McCarthy's work. His first novel, *The Orchard Keeper*, won the Faulkner prize for best first novel, and for his fourth novel, *Suttree*, McCarthy was critically acclaimed as the first novelist since World War II who could merit comparison to Faulkner.

In McCarthy's writing, we hear the echoes of Faulkner's unique language. It is the language of the South, of poetry, of the

Bible, filled with images of legends and myths. McCarthy also shares much with Faulkner's philosophy: the earth and simple people endure, and, after disaster, we will still hear the human voice, talking. In style, McCarthy is forming his own special voice. We hear the language of Faulkner, eloquent, but McCarthy's is a new version, bilingual and western, without stream of consciousness.

In theme, the adventure to a foreign country where war has altered the culture is similar to Hemingway's World War I and Spanish Civil War works *Farewell to Arms* and *For Whom the Bell Tolls*. Although John Grady and Rawlins do not fight in a war themselves, their lives are forever altered, not only by World War II, but by the Mexican Revolution, which took place 40 years before their adventure. Other echoes of Hemingway appear in the masculine skill with the wilderness and horses that both John Grady and Rawlins possess (John Grady is called one of the best riders alive by his friends, and his process is well confirmed by McCarthy's descriptions).

In addition, from Hemingway, McCarthy gets inspiration for his characters. Men of few words who camp, hunt, and fish, men who have their own codes and try to do right, be brave, and perform with grace—these are the characters who influence McCarthy's cowboys in the Border Trilogy books. In John Grady and Rawlins' sidekick, Blevins, who joins the two boys near the border, we find a quite Faulknerian character, one who brings to the novel humor as well as danger, with his tenacious single-mindedness.

Finally, when noting the influences of other writers on McCarthy's work, we cannot overlook Mark Twain's *The Adventures of Huckleberry Finn*. The similarities are striking: A young boy runs away from home to seek adventure and fortune, and, in the process, he must mature, grow, and learn to survive in a world different from the one he imagined.

A brief comment on language and culture in *All the Pretty Horses*. Cormac McCarthy, in this first novel of the Border Trilogy, uses numerous Spanish words and phrases. Most often, these words are clear to the careful reader, because he either repeats the word in English or explains the meaning before or after he uses it in Spanish. However, many other instances of Spanish phrases are not explained by surrounding English text. In those instances, readers may succeed at trying to decipher the text by looking for clues in English. For example, at the beginning of Chapter I, John Grady, at this point still only identified as "he," says to the cook, "I appreciate you lightin the candle," and when she replies "Como?" (meaning "why?") he says, "La candela. La vela." Readers can infer from her use of "no" in one phrase and "antes" in a following one that someone else lit the candle, a "senora" who was up before her. ("Ante" is used to mean "before" in many English words. For example, an "antecedent" is a preceding event or condition.) Here is another example that is somewhat easier to decipher. In the beginning of Chapter II, when John Grady is negotiating with the manager of the hacienda to try to break the sixteen wild horses they have found in a pen, the reader understands that the Spanish words refer to the horses. The conversations before and after this brief meeting make it clear that the two young American cowboys are planning to break the horses in four days. Although readers may not know the direct translation of the Spanish, much of it is clear from the context of the surrounding English text. Keep in mind that *All the Pretty Horses* is set in west Texas and Mexico, so many of the characters, including John Grady, are bilingual, speaking both English and Spanish. *All the Pretty Horses* is written from a dual-cultural, if not multicultural, context; the language directs us to this point of view.

In addition to the Spanish terminology that may be unfamiliar to many readers, McCarthy uses cowboy terminology, especially references to specific kinds of tack (horse equipment). Names of plants and grasses of the southwest desert region are also found throughout the text. (In order to explain these phrases in more detail, a glossary is provided at the end of every Commentary section, for your reference.)

A comment on the Border Trilogy. The books of Cormac McCarthy's Border Trilogy, in order of publication, are *All the Pretty Horses, The Crossing,* and *Cities of the Plain.* But the books are not a story in sequence and are not sequential even in theme. Rather, they are three pieces of a large puzzle, a picture of the American Southwest, specifically an area of the border with Mexico that runs from Laredo, Texas, to Tucson, Arizona. McCarthy is presenting a picture of that vast desert, grassland, and mountain region where the last of the pioneers settled.

The three books can be read in any order because each enhances the story and expands upon the themes of the others. *The Crossing* is in many ways parallel to *All the Pretty Horses*. The main character in *The Crossing*, Billy Parham, goes to Mexico the first time alone, to take a pregnant, injured wolf back to its home in the mountains after its mate has been killed. Parham begins this difficult task at the end of the 1930s and is away for some time. When he returns, his parents have been murdered and six horses stolen. So he leaves with his younger brother, Boyd, to return to Mexico and retrieve the horses. Billy (about 17 years old) and Boyd (almost 15 years old) travel several weeks and find the horses, but they lose most of the horses again, and Boyd is wounded on their return trip. Billy finds a kind old doctor who saves Boyd's life, but Boyd insists on Billy going to find the young girl who had accompanied them on part of their journey in Mexico. After he is well, Boyd and the girl run away together, and Billy travels around for several months and can't find them. So finally, he returns to the United States alone. World War II has begun, and he tries to enlist but is rejected several times for a minor heart defect. He decides to return to Mexico after finding one of their horses at a ranch; instead of finding Boyd, he finds Boyd's grave. Billy digs up his brother's body and brings his remains home.

In *Cities of the Plain*, Billy Parham and John Grady Cole (the main character in *All the Pretty Horses*) meet up on a New Mexican ranch not far from El Paso. The first scene of the novel shows the two men, with a third cowboy, drinking at a bar in Juarez across the border from El Paso. Billy calls John Grady the all-American cowboy. We never see the character Rawlins from *All the Pretty Horses* again, and at the end of *Cities of the Plain*, we find out that John Grady has not contacted his family around San Angelo for three years, since the end of the *Pretty Horses* saga.

In *Cities of the Plain*, McCarthy provides more stories of ranching life. John Grady rides the range checking cattle and notices a small calf that runs with a strange gait. He ropes and throws the calf, ties it up, and discovers a broken-off small piece of wood pushed into the calf's inner leg. By pushing and finally using his teeth, he extracts the piece of wood. Meanwhile, the wound is infected, so he swabs it with antiseptic, which he carries in his saddlebag. In this scene, we learn why roping was such an important skill in the raising of cattle on the range. If John Grady hadn't roped and treated the calf, it would have died from the infection. In this final novel in the trilogy, John Grady is still admired and known for his expertise with horses. When a wealthy man is looking for someone to train his filly so that he can give the horse to his wife for a present, the ranch owner recommends John Grady for the job. John Grady rejects the horse because it has an invisible crack in one hoof that someone has tried to cover up. He knows the horse is lame because it twitches one ear when it steps on that hoof. The men try to bribe John Grady to keep the horse but he makes them put it back in the truck and leave.

Even as an older young adult, John Grady still has an idealistic streak. He falls in love with a young girl who is different from the rest and starts to fix up a remote cabin on the ranch so that they can marry. He also has a very wild, half-ruined horse that he is determined to turn around. None of the other cowboys believes he can tame the horse, but John Grady proves them wrong.

At the end of *Cities of the Plain*, we find Billy Parham in his late seventies, wandering in Arizona at the end of the 1900s. The cities of this final novel in the trilogy are the border towns, El Paso and Juarez. Many scholars note the similarities to the biblical "cities of the plain" where Abraham and Lot settled, the cities of Sodom and Gomorrah. To be sure, in the last novel of the trilogy, more corruption is present than in the first two books.

The end is near and the image of John Grady on his horse, horse and rider appearing as one, is soon to be extinct. Man's connection with nature, his oneness with it, is at an end.

A BRIEF SYNOPSIS

Set in west Texas about 125 miles from the Mexican border near Del Rio and Langtry, *All the Pretty Horses* is a story of loss and adventure. John Grady Cole, the main character, is just 16 years old and attending his grandfather's funeral when the novel opens. His mother and father are finally divorcing after years of separation, and his mother is determined to sell the ranch owned by her father. So John Grady sets off on his horse, Redbo, accompanied by his best friend Lacey Rawlins, on his horse, Junior. They ride south across Texas, and, just north of the border, an even younger runaway boy follows them on a big bay horse. Rawlins, the realist, thinks Blevins, who has named himself after a radio preacher, will be nothing but trouble; John Grady, the idealist, is more sympathetic. Sticking together, the three boys ride their horses naked across the Rio Grande River, after securing their belongings in their tied-up pants.

In a lightning thunderstorm, Blevins loses everything except one boot, but a few days later, when they see his horse in a small town, Encantada, the three of them dare to reclaim it, but, of course, they are followed. Blevins separates from John Grady and Rawlins, who finally arrive at a beautiful hacienda that they have heard about on their journey. They find work as cowboys and wranglers, breaking sixteen wild mustangs in four days, to earn their reputations. Soon, because John Grady has proved his abilities with horses, he is promoted to breeder for Senor Rocha, the hacienda owner. A love story begins when the owner's daughter, Alejandra, a year older than John Grady, seduces him. Rawlins tries to warn his friend of the danger he is getting into by entering a relationship with the owner's daughter. The two boys are taken away in handcuffs at the end of Chapter II, when they are caught by the men who saw them take Blevins' horse back and accused of stealing.

Rawlins is very angry with John Grady, who defends himself by saying that some things (meaning passionate love affairs) aren't reasonable. After several days of hard riding, John Grady and Rawlins are put in a small jail cell in an adobe building and find Blevins there with broken feet. A fourth dweller in the cell, an old man, tells the boys that Blevins has killed three men, but Blevins says only one of the men died. After earning money on a farm for two months, Blevins went back to Encantada to retrieve his pistol. Having his horse was not enough for Blevins, and his return to the town where he retrieved his horse has now jeopardized three lives (his own, John Grady's, and Rawlins'). During a transfer south to Saltillo prison, Blevins is shot and killed in the woods. John Grady and Rawlins, after much fighting in the Saltillo prison yard, are both severely wounded. Finally, John Grady is given an envelope of money by the commandant, and they are released. They figure out that Duena Alfonsa, the great aunt of Alejandra, the young girl John Grady loves, has bought their freedom.

Rawlins decides to go home to Texas by way of Nuevo Larado, but John Grady wants to see Alejandra and also try to get their horses back. Rawlins is afraid for John Grady, who reassures him that he is not Blevins. John Grady makes it to La Purisima where the great aunt tells John Grady that Alejandra has promised never to see him again in turn for her great-aunt sending the money to release him from prison. The great-aunt, Duena Alfonsa, also tells John Grady how he has disappointed Senor Rocha by lying and denying any knowledge of Blevins. John Grady claims he wasn't allowed to tell his side of the story, but she says that does not matter. She gives him a horse and he rides to Torreon where he calls Alejandra in Mexico City. She agrees to meet him in Zacatecas, and they both take trains to meet there. Despite their love and his entreaties, she refuses to marry him. He gets drunk but makes his way back to Torreon and the grullo horse, the wild one he first broke with Rawlins a few months before.

At a crossroads while riding north, John Grady turns around and goes to the town where he was first jailed and, by taking the captain hostage, he retrieves his horse (Redbo), Rawlins' horse (Junior), and Blevins' big bay. He has to let the wonderful grullo go, because it is not strong enough for the long trip. But he manages to cross into Texas, again near Langtry, the area of Judge Roy Bean, where he travels for several months, trying to find the rightful owner of the bay. A judge helps him when some degenerates try to claim the horse. The judge listens to John Grady's story and assures him that the man he killed in prison and the captain who jailed them in the small town are not good people. The judge tries to urge John Grady to go easier on himself.

In Del Rio, Texas, John Grady visits the real Jimmy Blevins, who has never heard of anyone fitting the boy's description and has never seen the horse. After feeding John Grady a big meal and telling him about the radio preaching business, the reverend goes off to write a sermon. John Grady rides back to San Angelo and goes to Rawlins' family place and whistles for his friend, who is delighted to see John Grady and his horse, Junior.

After attending, on the sidelines, the funeral of the old woman, Abuela, who had done most of the work raising him, John Grady rides west, a lonely figure on one horse, leading his second mount.

LIST OF CHARACTERS

John Grady Cole

The protagonist of the novel; the main character around whom most of the story revolves. He is a disenfranchised 16-year-old who cannot save his family ranch, which is his rightful legacy. In Mexico, when he finds another ranch and falls in love with the only child of that hacienda's owner, he works very hard to prove himself, in the hopes of perhaps making a future there, but his plan fails. John Grady is attractive (his friend calls him a "ladies man"), smart, and highly skilled with horses. He believes in right and wrong, and is passionate not only about horses and his beloved but also about his ideas.

Lacey Rawlins

John Grady's best friend. He runs away from home with John Grady but worries about being followed and, eventually, wonders what his family and friends are doing back home (where he remains at the novel's end). More sentimental than John Grady, Rawlins is also more realistic. He believes that Blevins is trouble, and yet, when Blevins is tortured and shot, Rawlins is terribly affected; he is the one who can't believe places like the Saltillo prison exist. His friendship and affection for John Grady and for his horse last throughout the novel.

Blevins, the kid

The 13-year-old (whose age is somewhat undetermined, because he lies so often) who sees John Grady and Rawlins in a town just north of the border and follows them. John Grady feels sorry for Blevins, and Blevins accompanies John Grady and Rawlins into Mexico. After landing in jail, he is tortured and shot.

Alejandra

The beautiful, dark-haired, 17-year-old daughter of the hacienda owner in Mexico. She rides a stylish black Arab horse English-style and speaks schoolbook English. She splits her time between Mexico City, where her mother lives, and La Purisima, her father's ranch. Alejandra seduces John Grady, who can refuse her nothing. Her great aunt arranges for the release of John Grady and Rawlins from prison and makes Alejandra promise never to see John Grady again. Alejandra does see John Grady in Zacatecas but refuses to run away and marry him. She is more bound by convention than her rebellious ways would indicate.

Senor Rocha, also called Don Hector

The 40-year-old owner of La Purisima hacienda. His family has owned the property for many years and he still lives on it, unlike many other rich landowners. He has an airplane, which he uses to fly to Mexico City where his wife resides. He loves horses and is fond of John Grady, recognizing John Grady's great skills.

Duena Alfonsa

The great aunt to Alejandra who lives at La Purisima and who loved Gustave Madero, one of the martyrs of the Mexican Revolution. She was the victim of a shooting accident when she was young and is missing two fingers on one hand. She plays chess with John Grady and is informative about the Revolution and other ideas. But she is very unbending and will not help John Grady win the right to be a part of Alejandra's life. She has decided what will be best and she, apparently, wields the power in the family. She does save John Grady's life, in exchange for the promise from Alejandra that she, Alejandra, will never see him again. She is an intelligent woman, with no sympathy.

Grandfather Grady

Never alive in the novel, he died too soon to pass the ranch on to his grandson. It is his funeral scene that begins the novel. A kind man who never let anyone speak ill of his daughter (John Grady's mother) and who refused to have a funeral until dog tags at least came home. "He never gave up," John Grady recounts to Cole.

Cole

The father of John Grady, a World War II veteran who was a prisoner of war. His marriage to John Grady's mother has failed.

He has made money in the oil fields and at gambling, but he makes no attempt to buy the ranch or resist his wife's divorce papers. He takes long horse rides with John Grady and tries to give him advice.

Mother

Never given a name, the mother of John Grady left him in the care of the Mexican women at the ranch and went to Los Angeles when he was a baby. She is now pursuing an acting career in San Antonio, has a young lover, and refuses to even lease the ranch to John Grady. She wants to sell it and take the money.

Redbo and Junior

The horses of John Grady and Rawlins, respectively; the two boys' best friends. After surviving the Mexican adventure, Junior ends up at home with Rawlins and Redbo with John Grady and the big bay heading west.

Mary Catherine

John Grady's girlfriend in San Angelo, Texas, who, at the start of the novel, has left him for another man.

Franklin

The lawyer John Grady consults in San Angelo about his parents' divorce and the ownership of the family ranch.

Luisa and Arturo

Along with Abuela, the old mother of Luisa, they have run the Grady ranch for years and lived there all their lives.

Armando, Antonio, and Maria

The servants who run the La Purisima hacienda. Antonio, who speaks no English, takes a truck all the way to Kentucky to bring back the chestnut stallion.

Captain

The man who comes to arrest John Grady and Rawlins and keeps them in a small jail cell. He is the one who cruelly shoots Blevins and whom John Grady later takes as a hostage in order to retrieve the American horses.

Perez

The man, who may or may not be a prisoner, but who has a small dwelling in the yard of the Saltillo prison and seems to run the workings inside the prison. He has power over the life and death of the prisoners.

The Judge (or Charles, as his wife Dixie calls him)

In Texas he restores the bay to John Grady's care after con artists try to claim it is theirs. He listens to John Grady's story, is kind, and gives good advice.

Reverend Jimmy Blevins

The radio preacher from Del Rio, Texas, who says he has never heard of the kid who has taken his name or of the big bay he is riding. He and his wife feed John Grady a wonderful meal and tell him about their life.

CRITICAL COMMENTARIES

CHAPTER I

Summary

A death vigil serves as the opening scene in *All the Pretty Horses*. It is the year 1949, and John Grady Cole has returned to the ranch for the wake of his grandfather. It is dark and cold in the early morning when he learns from the housekeeper that his mother is also in the house. Wearing a black suit, John Grady walks down a hallway where portraits of his ancestors hang. A candle lights the room where his grandfather is laid in funeral cloth. The only sounds are a clock ticking and the whistle of a train. He goes to the kitchen and has coffee with Luisa.

At the funeral John Grady sees his father. A storm is brewing, with spits of snow and lots of wind, which cause the preacher's words to be lost. That evening John Grady saddles his horse for a ride near the old Comanche road, which comes down from the Kiowa country on the western section of the ranch. He returns in the dark.

McCarthy provides John Grady's family history, and we finally learn the protagonist's name. The house in which John Grady grew up was built in 1872. The original 1866 ranch had 2,300 acres; the first house was one room made of sticks and wattle. The grandfather was the oldest of eight boys, the only one to live past the age of 25 and the first to die in the house. The Grady surname dies with the old man.

John Grady meets his father in the lobby of a hotel in town, and they go to the Eagle Cafe to eat. His father has little appetite and smokes too much, according to his son, who chastises him for the habit. They arrange a horseback ride for Saturday. In the next scene John Grady and his friend Rawlins have returned from a ride and are discussing John Grady's mother, who has a boyfriend only two years older than John Grady. He rubs down his horse and goes to the kitchen for coffee. Then John Grady enters the study of his grandfather. His mother comes down the stairs and asks him what he is doing and he replies, "Settin."

He spends some afternoons talking with his father about why he didn't buy the ranch. The father at one time had money from work in the oil rigs and gambling but wasted it all. He is a veteran of World War II and hasn't spoken to John Grady's mother for seven years. The father gives John Grady a Hamley Formfitter saddle.

John Grady stays on the ranch with Luisa and Arturo after his mother returns to San Antonio and her acting engagements. When she returns, John Grady tries to get her to lease him the ranch. She says it hasn't paid for 20 years and that he has to go to school. John Grady goes to see a lawyer named Franklin who does not give him any hope about the ranch. They also talk about John Grady's father's ill health.

After Christmas, when his mother is away most of the time, John Grady hitchhikes to San Antonio to see her in the play she is appearing in. He does not let her know he is there, but he watches her from behind a newspaper with her young boyfriend in the lobby of the Menger Hotel.

In March, he takes a last ride with his father. They discuss horses, John Grady's girlfriend, and John Grady's future. His father provides some explanation of his marriage to John Grady's mother as well as their divorce. The father wants John Grady to make up with his mother. Closing on the ranch sale is scheduled to take place June 1. John Grady and his friend Rawlins make plans to run away on their horses. He sees his girlfriend, Mary Catherine, for the last time.

The last two-thirds of Chapter I follow the two young men on their horses to the border at Langtry and tell of their ride approximately 170 miles into Mexico to a large hacienda where they seek work as cowboys.

Their journey is filled with the details of riding and camping and finding food and water. Their brief discussions are often about horses and women.

A raggedy kid on a big horse attaches himself to John Grady and Rawlins. Rawlins wants to leave him, but John Grady is kinder, even though he joins Rawlins in teasing the country kid.

After their food supply is depleted, they occasionally buy food. But they also rely on the kindness of strangers. In one scene, they are invited to dinner with a Mexican family. The two little girls in the family enjoy laughing at Blevins when he leans back and falls off the bench at the table.

The three boys get some fermented drink from some migrant traders, which makes them very drunk and sick. They leave to continue their journey.

A storm comes and Blevins is afraid of lightning and tells stories about his relatives who have been struck dead. He tries to outride the storm. John Grady and Rawlins find him the next morning, naked except for undershorts. He has removed all of his clothes so that he is wearing no metal and will not attract lightning. His horse and pistol are gone, and all his clothes, except one boot, have washed away.

In a dangerous and comic scene, the three boys recover the horse they find in a village. Water becomes even more of a problem than it has been in the past, and the horses start to suffer. John Grady and Rawlins split ways with Blevins, whose horse is stronger; Blevins tries to get the pursuers to follow him.

Finally, John Grady and Rawlins come upon grass that has been described to them as part of a beautiful hacienda. The vaqueros, or cowboys, tending the cattle let them follow along, and the foreman takes them to the manager's house. A young girl in English riding gear rides by from the marsh on a black Arabian horse. John Grady and Rawlins are hired on and sleep in the bunkhouse.

Commentary

The major characters of Chapter I are John Grady Cole, his best friend Rawlins, his parents, and his grandfather. But the sidekick Blevins, the landscape (as noted by others), and the horses are also major players in the story. McCarthy's descriptions of the land, vegetation, and wildlife impart to the novel a tone and texture that frames the events and the characters.

The theme of nature is strong. The sense of place imbues the characters, especially John Grady, with a masculinity that makes them larger than life and certainly more significant than labels like "cowboy" or "macho." John Grady is talented and skilled — lucky enough to be doing what he was born to do. When John Grady rides, he is one with the horse. This ease is seen clearly when he takes one foot out of its stirrup, leans over on the other side, and picks up Blevins' hat, never slowing his horse and always maintaining the gait.

John Grady loves the land, and the first great tragedy of the story is the fact that his family's ranch will be sold after his grandfather's death. In analyzing the causes of the sale of the ranch, we see a changing world where a horse culture is dying. World War II is one of the villains of the story, because it has left John Grady's father unable to take charge not only of his own life and marriage, but also of the ranch.

John Grady's mother is an actress playing at a theater in San Antonio in a play that disappoints John Grady because it tells him nothing about the way the world "was or was becoming." His mother is determined to get rid of the ranch, and she refuses to let John Grady lease it or become any part of it. All of the Mexican workers at the ranch will have to leave as well.

In this chapter, we find out that John Grady's parents are only recently divorced, although they have been separated for nearly John Grady's entire life. His mother may have planned to sell her father's property after his death all along. We know that the lawyer John Grady consults says there is nothing to be done, and that same lawyer had warned John Grady's father about signing the divorce papers because he knew that to do so would be to give up his rights to the land. So both of John Grady's parents may be partially responsible for the outcome.

But we must also wonder about the role of John Grady's grandfather in the unfortunate conclusion to the family ranch. We know that he defended both his son-in-law and his daughter — the daughter in fights against gossipers and the son-in-law when he was reported missing in the war. How could such a man with so much caring for his family, of whom everyone is so fond, not plan for the ranch's future? Was he unable to plan for the future because he was paralyzed by the deaths of his seven younger brothers? Did he not know what to do with his land because he had no sons? He must have known his daughter would not keep the ranch, and how could he *not* see his son-in-law's problems and weaknesses? Did it occur to him to provide for his namesake, his grandson John Grady? Perhaps fatalism plays a role in the grandfather's indifference. Often, one hears a defeated, aging person say, "Well, I don't care what happens to this ranch, or farm, after I die." The Grady family story is a warning to others that if you love the land, you must plan for its future. The American Dream isn't just about acquiring land and fortune and assuming that it will be passed down as one wishes to the next generation. The land, and ownership of it, is a trust; providing for its future is as important as proper grazing techniques and keeping up the fences. Indeed, the American Dream should not just be about providing money for one's heirs. The greatest legacy would be to save the land for future generations' contented enjoyment. Apparently, Grandfather Grady did not have the vision to do this.

So Chapter I begins not only with a wake and a funeral in the cold of winter shortly before Christmas, but also with the impending loss of the ranch. The significance of the ranch is not its size; what matters is that it carries the entire history of John Grady's family, from the moment his great grandfather first came to America. John Grady tries valiantly to save the ranch. He hitchhikes to San Antonio to observe his mother, to try to understand her and find a way, then, to change her mind. He talks, not only to the lawyer, but to both of his parents, to no avail. Now the ranch will be acquired by an oil company, or worse, and who knows what will become of it.

Another significant loss in John Grady's life is the marriage of his parents. His father tells him that he and John Grady's mother shared a love of horses and says he thought that was enough. Obviously, and unfortunately, it was not. The freedom with which John Grady's mother leaves her family to pursue acting — and a younger male companion — is very unusual for the era. This loss of his parents' marriage — and of a cohesive family — prophesies the great fracture that would occur in American life with shocking percentages starting about 20 years after the novel takes place. More importantly, it foreshadows problems with which John Grady will struggle in his own life. Rawlins tells John Grady that women aren't worth it, but John Grady replies, "Yes, they are." However, even with his optimism about women, the problem of love and making a workable relationship are ones that John Grady will struggle with in the last half of *All the Pretty Horses* and *Cities of the Plain*, the third of McCarthy's trilogy and the sequel to John Grady Cole's story.

After the somewhat bizarre funeral of his grandfather, with the lawn chairs blowing about and the minister's words lost, John Grady Cole saddles his horse in the evening's long shadows and rides one of many solitary rides, to the western edge of the ranch where he imagines a past with painted ponies and riders of the lost nation, pledged in blood, as he dreams the scene. He thinks that when the wind is in the north he can hear them, the breath of the horses and their hooves shod in rawhide. He pictures in his mind a complete scene, from dogs and children and women to the giant serpent-like marks in the sand from their dragging travois poles. He hears their song and mourns their short and violent lives.

Although the negative themes of death, loss of family and love relationships, and a change in the land are critical in *All the Pretty*

Horses, some positive themes do hold their own. The first of these positive themes is friendship. The bond between Rawlins and John Grady extends beyond their similar problems with their families; they are complements to each. John Grady is the more skilled, honorable, and idealistic of the two — and probably the brightest. But Rawlins gives him perfect dialogue, not only in their discussions of life and death, but in their undertakings. Rawlins is the realist, the survivor, who is always slightly cynical. He tries to moderate John Grady's excesses, and even if he does not succeed, they always consult each other when solving a problem. John Grady and Rawlins have been successful in their journey and survived and reached the place they were searching for. McCarthy says, "The vaqueros knew them by the way they sat their horses and they called them caballero." This is significant, because "caballero" is the highest designation for a cowboy or rider. "Caballero" has connotations of hero, just like the American best use of "cowboy." And the word derives from gentleman, which adds to the distinction in Spanish culture. A vaquero is also a highly skilled horseman or cowboy, but not quite as highly regarded, yet superior to a trainer of horses. In the United States, "cowboy" often has a higher designation than "wrangler" or "horse handler," but now sometimes it has a derogatory meaning. Not so with caballero and vaquero. So, by making this long trip and by how they sit their horses, the Mexican vaqueros have given high praise to John Grady and Rawlins by calling them "caballero."

Above all else, *All the Pretty Horses* is an adventure story. It is this journey, started in Chapter I, that helps both of the young men to mature. John Grady begins the story as the 16-year-old boy who arrives at the ranch dressed in a black suit, trying to be grown up for his grandfather's funeral. When he views the body, he says, "That was not sleeping," as though he were a child who has been told that death is a sleep and who must grow up and face what death really is.

(Here and in the following sections, difficult words, phrases, and colloquialisms are explained.)

- **waisted cutglass vase** a vase ornamented with patterns cut into the glass, considered valuable as an antique; "waisted" here apparently

refers to the shape, usually called "hourglass," but either McCarthy likes to humanize important objects or this is a southern expression.
- **Buenos diás, guapo**   (Spanish) Good morning, handsome guy.
- **Cómo?**   (Spanish) What?
- **la vela**   (Spanish) the candle.
- **No fui yo**   (Spanish) It wasn't me.
- **la señora**   (Spanish) the mistress (of the house) or Mrs.
- **claro**   (Spanish) of course.
- **Ya se levantó?**   (Spanish) She's already up?
- **antes que yo**   (Spanish) before me.
- **Comanch, Kiowa**   Native American Indian tribes who were located in the central and western plains of the United States.
- **grail**   object of endeavor. The holy grail was the cup Jesus drank from at the Last Supper and the object of the knights' medieval quests (searches or journeys).
- **die-up**   cowboy language for a big loss of livestock.
- **Palmer Feed and Supply blotter**   a heavy piece of almost felt-like paper, approximately 18 inches square, which protects the wood on a desk and is used to blot the ink of writing when using an old-fashioned ink well and pen. An old western practice of feed stores was to give good customers presents at Christmas. Today, feed store memorabilia is considered quite valuable and includes household utensils that are inscribed.
- **Good Book**   the Christian Bible.
- **Hamley Formfitter saddle**   Hamley was a respected and prominent saddle maker of the era before and during the novel. The term "formfitter" designated a type of saddle where the cantle (the swells at the rear of the saddle) were very high and almost tight fitting, making it more difficult for the rider to fall out of the saddle. However, if the saddle was not custom fitted to the owner, it might have been too difficult for the rider to get into or out of the saddle.
- **Algo más?**   (Spanish) Anything else?
- **Buenas noches**   (Spanish) Good night.
- **Andalusian**   an ancient breed of horses from Andalucian, Spain; often gray, but also black or bay (reddish brown) in color. Many horse breeds

can be traced to these high-stepping horses, including the Lipizzaner. The Spaniards brought these horses to North and South America, where such breeds as the Mustang, Criollo, Paso Fino, and Appaloosa can trace an Andalusian lineage.

- **Barb** an ancient breed of horse originating in Algeria and Morocco known for their toughness and stamina; may also be quick-tempered. These horses may date back to prehistoric times and have similarities with the Arabian horse, with which they have been crossbred since the Muslims invaded the north coast of Africa. However, the Barb has a broader head than the Arabian horse, and slopping hindquarters as well. The foundation horses of England and America can be traced back to this Barb horse. Most horse breeds have mixed lineage, with some breeds having been crossbred more than others. The Barb is a horse with certain strong physical features, but it was not bred purely until quite recently. In contrast, the Arab has been purebred for centuries and is perhaps one of the few breeds that one could rightly call purebred. This subject is a confusing one, even to horse fanciers, because a horse can be registered in a breed, depending on its lineage and its characteristics. Many horses are registered as part of a distinct breed, but they may not be "pure" at all.
- **Steeldust** a famous stallion in 19th century Texas; a legendary bay quarter horse that came from Kentucky and sired many horses for the old Texas foundation horses.
- **cutting horse** a western horse bred for cutting, or separating, cattle from the herd. These horses can move very quickly, make exceptional sharp turns, and spin around on one back hoof to close in on a wayward steer or cow. The best cutting horses are known for being, as the cowboys say, "cowy"; that is, they are attracted to cattle and are interested in moving in close and shoving them into place.
- **Más cafe?** (Spanish) More coffee?
- **Sí por favor** (Spanish) Yes, please.
- **Hace much frío** (Spanish) It is very cold.
- **Bastante** (Spanish) That's enough. (Here, this probably refers to filling the coffee cup and not to the weather, although it may be referring to both.)
- **closing** a real estate term for the day when all papers are signed in the sale of a piece of property.
- **soogan** bedroll; derivation may be Native American.

- **catspaw** a tool for grabbing that has one or more hooks.
- **gyp water** containing gypsum and, thus, calcium.
- **javelina** wild pig.
- **bajada** (Spanish) drop; slope.
- **gunsel** goose or criminal.
- **Colt Bisley with guttapercha grips** Colt revolvers were the popular guns that won the West. Guttapercha is a hard rubber-like material from a Malaysian tree. This gun handle, or grip, is made of that material.
- **nopal** prickly pear cactus of which many varieties exist. The fruits of many varieties of nopal are edible, and the beaver-tail shaped pads, found in some varieties, also make good food.
- **creosote** a shrub of the desert southwest with small leaves and a pungent smell. Also called greasewood and chaparral. Used as a cancer treatment by the Native Americans.
- **tienda** (Spanish) store.
- **Tiene also que tomar?** (Spanish) Do you have anything to drink?
- **Buenas tardes** (Spanish) Good afternoon.
- **retablo** an artwork often fashioned of tin.
- **Deben comer** (Spanish) You ought to eat.
- **bizcochos** Mexican biscuits or hard rolls.
- **cordilleras** (Spanish) chain of mountains.
- **sideoats grama** a short pasture grass that is very resilient and makes decent nutrition for cattle and horses.
- **Basketgrass** a native grass to the Americas, used in making baskets.
- **Lechugilla** a large wild lettuce, shaped from a crown, like a century plant.
- **kiacks** baskets hung at the side of pack animals.
- **Son de Tejas?** (Spanish) Are you (plural) from Texas?
- **buena suerte** (Spanish) good luck.
- **candelilla** large-leaved plants used to make wax.
- **cholla** a desert cactus of which there are many varieties, most with terrible stickers, but often beautiful in their miniature tree shapes.

- **Qué vale?** (Spanish) What is it worth?
- **Es mucho trabajo** (Spanish) It is a lot of work.
- **Es su hermano, el rubio?** (Spanish) Is he your brother, the blonde?
- **Quién es?** (Spanish) Who is he?
- **un muchacho, no más** (Spanish) a kid, no more.
- **Algún parentesco?** (Spanish) Any kinship?
- **un amigo** (Spanish) a friend.
- **pollarded mountains** mountains with the peaks cut off.
- **hackamore** a horse bridle that has no bit and uses a rope fitting around the top of the horse's nose, about four inches up from the muzzle. Knots at the side of the nose attach to the reins. The horse is controlled because, when the reins are pulled, the hackamore shuts off the horse's air by tightening around the nose. The side knots, if positioned carefully, can also press sensitive nerves to help control the horse. Without extra equipment, John Grady and Rawlins are fashioning this bridle so that Blevins can still ride bareback.
- **ocotillo** a Sonorean desert plant, not a cactus, but with tall, thin, pole-like branches that fan out from the base. These poles have very small green leaves all over when the plant has received enough rain, and the tops form six-inch, flag-like, orange-red flowers. The poles make excellent fences.
- **paloverde** a southwestern tree about four to eight feet tall. The name means green stick. These trees have no leaves unless they receive rain, in which case they become covered with fern-like greenery and flowers. They can photosynthesize from their bark and stems and can live for extremely long periods without water.
- **caballero** (Spanish) vernacular for "cowboy"; also, originally, "gentleman who travels by horse"; here, both meanings apply.
- **ciénagas** (Spanish) swamp or marsh.
- **gaited rack** a little trot. A good saddle horse can perform two walks, two trots, a rack, two lopes or canters, as well as a gallop.
- **caporal** (Spanish) foreman.
- **gerente** (Spanish) manager.
- **güeros** (Spanish) fighter.

CHAPTER II

Summary

John Grady's last words in Chapter I are that he wants to stay at La Purisima hacienda for "about a hundred years." The hacienda is a large ranch covering about 26,000 acres in the Mexican state of Coahuila. The area has desert as well as grasslands and is edged on the west by the Sierras, where some elevations are as high as 9,000 feet. Natural springs and lagunas, or lakes, provide adequate water. La Purisima is one of the few haciendas left in Mexico where the owner, Don Hector (also called Rocha) a descendant of the original owner, still lives on the estate. His wife lives in Mexico City, and he flies an airplane back and forth between residences. Don Hector runs a thousand head of cattle and loves horses. He has a pack of silver greyhounds and brings friends to go hunting. Rawlins observes that they have no guns, and John Grady thinks they are going to hunt coyotes with ropes. Don Hector is a gentleman sportsman. The greyhounds for hunting and the observation that the men are probably hunting coyotes with ropes shows that his relation to nature, and thus, the horses, is different from John Grady's. John Grady would hunt a coyote if it were necessary because the coyote was killing calves, for example. Don Hector, on the other hand, entertains himself with and uses creatures for sporting purposes.

John Grady and Rawlins begin working, branding, marking, castrating, and dehorning cattle. On the third day, the vaqueros, or Mexican cowboys, bring in a small herd of wild colts from the mesa. They are of varied size, conformation, and color and spook easily. John Grady guesses that they have never seen human beings, and Rawlins says that the horses are worthless. John Grady argues with him and says that there are a few good ones. He points out the head on one horse. Rawlins says, "You used to be awful particular about horses." John Grady nods, and replies, "Well, I aint forgot what they're supposed to look like." They both think that the one thing going for the horses is that they have not been broken by the Mexicans, not because they do not come to respect some of the vaqueros, but because they know that a horse broken incorrectly is harder to fix than starting with a very wild, but untouched, horse.

John Grady suggests that they try to break these sixteen horses in four days. His idea is to end up with "just halfway decent green-broke horses." They will sideline the horses, which requires a lot of rope (see the following Commentary section for more information on the methods of breaking horses). Armando, one of the ranch workers, has reported that there are maybe four hundred head of horses on the mountain — medium bloods, or quarterhorses. John Grady observes the horses and suggests that the bloodlines come from some famous horses sold from Texas into Mexico.

John Grady and Rawlins go to the kitchen and talk to the manager. He doesn't think they will be able to break these horses using this method, but he does not forbid them to do it. So, the next day, they begin the hobbling and sacking of the horses. Rawlins assists John Grady, who says, "No such thing as a mean colt." John Grady floats a gunnysack over the horse's face and rubs the sack over it, all the while talking to the horse. These gunnysacks carry John Grady's scent because he slept on them the night before. Rawlins asks, "What good do you think it does to waller all over a horse thataway?" John Grady's reply is, "I dont know. I aint a horse."

Because they have little equipment, except ropes, they make hackamore bridles. They begin at daybreak, and, by dark, John Grady has ridden eleven of the horses. By the end of the second day, John Grady and Rawlins have both ridden all the horses.

On the first morning, the Mexican cowboys come to watch and, by the afternoon, women and children have also gathered. By the fourth morning, John Grady is ready to ride one of the horses out of the pen. In the afternoon, he rides the grullo that Rawlins had chosen as the wildest of the bunch. On the ride, the young girl Alejandra, the daughter of Rocha, rides by him on her black Arabian horse. John Grady wants to speak but doesn't. That evening the manager and another hand come to inspect the horses. Antonio, of the vaqueros, rides two of the horses. At supper, they receive even more deference from the other vaqueros than they had on the first day.

Three days later they are sent into the mountains with three young Mexican cowboys and an old man who cooks for them. They each have a string of three horses to carry equipment. Their job is to hunt and bring back more wild horses. The old man fought in the Mexican Revolution and loves horses. He talks to them in the evening about the souls of horses.

After three weeks of work they have eight mares trapped in a stone ravine made to hold the horses. When they return, John Grady meets with Don Hector, who says he has heard that John Grady understands horses. John Grady's only reply is, "I been aroun em some." Don Hector chats with him about John Grady's age and the age of Rawlins and observes that John Grady is the leader. John Grady says, "We dont have no leaders. We're just buddies." Then they discuss horses over coffee, and Don Hector says that he wants to breed his own special quarterhorses from these wild mustang mares, with a stallion he has purchased, sight unseen, at an auction in Lexington, Kentucky. In their discussion, it is revealed that both Don Hector and John Grady think that the sire and the mare are of equal importance in producing a good horse, whereas many breeders think the sire is most important.

Because of the impression John Grady made upon Don Hector, he is to move from the bunkhouse to his own room in the barn and oversee the breeding of the horses. He discusses this with Rawlins, because he is worried about the breakup of the two buddies. Rawlins tells him it is an opportunity he can't ignore.

John Grady moves into the barn, built in the English style, with a cupola; the only other person living in the barn is a very old man who comes out the first day, looks at John Grady's horse, and says nothing. Later, he sees the old man pulling the cinchstrap on the black Arabian horse of Alejandra, who turns to look at John Grady and says, "Good afternoon." She gets on the horse and rides out of the barn.

That night, as John Grady is drifting off to sleep, he thinks about horses and the open country, especially wild horses. He thinks about these horses who have never seen a human being and "yet in whose souls he would come to reside forever."

He and Rawlins and two vaqueros go into the mountains to look for horses again, and they talk on their journey. Rawlins thinks the girl is a fancy sort and John Grady tells him she's not. John Grady has "readyrolls" he has gotten from La Vega, the nearby town. These rolls are a treat, because they are yeast rolls from a bakery, ready to eat or ready to reheat. Most of the time, they have been eating flat tortillas. After returning from the mountains, they go into the town on Sunday, riding horses they've been working on. They race each other on the horses, and, even when they exchange horses, John Grady wins. Their hair has been cut with sheepshears at the hacienda, and now they go to a store to buy some new clothes. John Grady convinces his friend to buy some black boots. They also get gloves, which they need in order to protect their hands.

The second half of Chapter II begins with a dance at a grange hall, which John Grady attends with Rawlins and a boy named Roberto from the ranch, at Alejandra's invitation. They share a small bottle of mescal. Alejandra is dancing with a tall boy from the San Pablo ranch. When she dances with John Grady, he finds her hands small and her waist slight. She speaks schoolbook English.

He rides home from the dance alone, and a fast-moving car passes him, causing his horse to get skittish. Left in the dust, he thinks the horse has done well, and he tells it so.

The stallion from Kentucky arrives after a long and complex trip made by Antonio, Armando's brother, who speaks no English. John Grady inspects the horse with Rocha and asks permission to ride the stallion. Then, for several days the two of them discuss the mares in the corral, John Grady arguing certain horses' merits. Rocha is the one who makes the final decision on which horse to breed with the stud, but he listens to John Grady's opinions. John Grady works with Antonio to breed the horses and conspires with him to tell Rocha the stallion needs to be ridden to keep it manageable, when in truth John Grady likes the girl to see him riding the powerful chestnut. He rides it to the end of the laguna and talks to it in Spanish, telling it he is the commander. Sometimes, on these early morning rides, he sees Alejandra riding.

John Grady starts to ride the horse bareback, just after breeding, and one day, coming out of the barn this way, he spots Alejandra on her Arab down the road. She stops and turns, asking to ride the stallion.

John Grady does what Alejandra asks and takes her Arabian horse back to Armando's, while she rides the stallion alone. Before she takes another trip to Mexico City, he sees her riding down from the mountains in the rain, and, to John Grady, she looks real and yet also like a dream.

While Alejandra is away, her great-aunt asks John Grady to play chess with her. They play on a board of circassian walnut and birdseye maple inlaid with pearl. The chess pieces are made of ivory and black horn. John Grady plays well against the old woman. They play late, and when tea is served he takes his black. On refusing the cake, crackers, and cheese, he says he'd "have crazy dreams eatin this late." She then discusses dreams with him and tells how she lost the last two fingers on her hand in a shooting accident, and she comments on the scar on his face and guesses, correctly, that he got it from a horse. She says, "Scars have the strange power to remind us that our past is real."

She informs him that Alejandra will be at the ranch for the summer, after a two-week stay in Mexico City. Then she talks about convention and the position of women, especially in Latin society. She tells him that she is the one who will get to say, and he responds that she didn't have to invite him just to tell him that. But she has the last word with, "It was because of that I almost didn't invite you."

In the next scene, he is discussing that evening with Rawlins, when they are camped under the stars. Rawlins asks him if he has eyes for the girl and the spread. To the latter John Grady does not know, but of Alejandra he says he can talk to her. Rawlins warns him that just because Rocha likes him doesn't mean he wants him for his daughter. Rawlins is worried they will get run off from the place. Also, John Grady is not sure if he has given his word to the great-aunt about what she asked. Here again there are class and culture clashes. The great-aunt has not asked John Grady anything specifically. She has said, "Here a woman's reputation is all she has." She has said, "I am the one who gets to say." Most of what she says implies some threat and a desire to protect Alejandra. But exactly what she wants either of the young people to do is quite unclear. The scene ends with John Grady saying she didn't have to invite him and the great-aunt says, "You're quite right." No wonder John Grady is confused and Rawlins is irritated.

Five nights later, Alejandra comes to John Grady's room to talk. They start to take night rides together, he on the stallion, she on her black Arab. One night, he leaves her, takes his clothes off, and goes swimming in the lake. She joins him. This begins their affair. She goes to his room every night for nine nights, and then she returns to Mexico City.

Rocha invites John Grady to play billiards in a room that was formerly the chapel for the hacienda. Rocha explains some of his views on the Revolution, the Maderos, and, thus, the great aunt's ideas. Later, John Grady imagines Alejandra in his room repeating the words he'd first said to her, "Tell me what to do. I'll do anything you say." But she is gone. Next, he is invited to Antonio's brother's house for dinner on Sunday. When he tells Antonio he intends to reveal to Alejandra his heart when she returns, he discovers that she has already returned.

He continues to work with the mares, and, two days later, he and Rawlins are in the mountains again. One night, three greyhounds come into their camp, but then they vanish and there are no other sounds.

After their return to the ranch, they are arrested in the middle of the night and taken on their horses to the north.

Commentary

Chapter II begins with Rawlins and John Grady working at La Purisima, and it appears they've found their paradise: jobs they love, a beautiful setting, a hacienda owner who is enlightened and loves horses, and a beautiful young girl who rides around on her black Arabian saddlehorse. John Grady is quickly promoted to breeder after their amazing feat of breaking sixteen wild mustangs in four days. The great-aunt of the girl invites John Grady to play chess, and he excels at that, too. Then the inevitable love affair, initiated by the dark, passionate girl, begins. But at the end of the chapter the two young men are dragged away at daybreak in handcuffs.

What happened to their almost perfect world? In the interview with Rocha, after the breaking of the horses and when John Grady is being considered for the horse breeding position, John Grady is asked if it was just the two of them who rode from Texas. For some unknown reason, John Grady, who is so honest about his abilities and in general very honorable, lies. He denies that Blevins had been with them. In the first chapter, Rawlins repeatedly warned John Grady that Blevins was trouble and that he would always reappear, but they have not seen him since the split-up after they retrieved Blevins' bay horse. So the chapter ends on this terrible unraveling, and the reader is eager to read on to find out for sure what has gone wrong and why Rawlins won't even look at his friend, John Grady.

But in the middle of the chapter is the heart of what the novel is really about — horses. The adventure, the love interest, the family histories, even the Mexican Revolution play second string to the horse lore and stories.

First, we read long scenes in which John Grady and Rawlins break the sixteen mustangs. The animals are so wild that John Grady says they do not smell like horses, they smell like wild animals. The horses are a varied lot in color, and some are spotted horses, or paints, which is reminiscent of Faulkner's short story "Spotted Horses." But here the boys are not pulling a con to sell the ponies; they are going to make them into decent riding or work horses for the ranch.

They use a method called sidelining to break the horses, which involves hobbling the horses so that when they kick and buck they fall down. In traditional bronc busting, a couple of cowboys catch and hold down a horse, putting a saddle on it. Then a brave "bronc-peeler," as Blevins had claimed to be, gets on and rides the bucking horse until it tires out and starts to run straight. This method of breaking horses can be witnessed at some rodeos where a "wild horse" division is put on. The work is dangerous, and, using this method, a totally unbroken horse is not really rideable for several weeks.

When the sidelining method is used (the method used by John Grady and Rawlins), a horse can be "greenbroke" in several days. The hobbling of the horse teaches it very quickly to stand without kicking. The horse also learns to walk without humping and dipping and lowering its head in preparation for a good buck. Simpler methods of sidelining exist than the method John Grady uses. Some of those methods involve just tying the back foot to the headpiece; another method ties the horse's neck around to the side. But John Grady does not have a lot of time, so he ties up all their legs with loose slipknots so that he can more quickly get these very unruly horses to stand and walk quietly.

The second part of John Grady's method is the sacking out. He drapes one of the gunnysacks he has slept on over the horse's face. For fifteen minutes, he rubs the horse with this sack and talks to it. He does this to build trust in the horse and so that the horse is less jittery about saddle blankets or the saddles that will be used on it. After this complex preparation, the first time John Grady gets on one of these horses, it just stands still, to the amazement of all the onlookers. Rawlins teases him that he is ruining the show, that this is not what everyone came to see. Of course, the audience expects John Grady to be bucked off right away.

John Grady is a precursor of the recent whisperers who have taken the horse gentler tradition and developed it into a third method of training horses, which has become popular in recent years, used by Monty Roberts and the movie *The Horse Whisperer*, which was very loosely based on Roberts' experience with a difficult, injured horse. This method involves going in a ring with a wild horse and bending down on one's haunches and very quietly getting eye contact with the horse. The trainer waits until the horse comes to him. Visual techniques are used to tame the horse, cues Roberts learned from watching horses. When the horse insists on a behavior the trainer does not want, the trainer, using the "whisperer" or visual technique, turns away from the horse until it starts again on the desired behavior. This shunning seems to work and is what mares use to control their young colts. The trainer also talks softly to the horse to encourage its trust and good behavior. Demonstrations of this method are put on all across the United States today. The current attention paid to this method does not give the credit it should to the long line of "amansadores" and gentlers, men like John Grady, who always use these methods of communing with horses. We see this when John Grady talks to the horses and in how they respond to his treatment.

The horse scenes add detail and interest to the story and provide a setting for the development of John Grady's character. The first time John Grady and Rawlins go into the mountains to catch horses, the old man who accompanies them recounts his own history and how he fought in the cavalry where his father and brothers had died. He tells them of the horses killed under him and how horses love war, just like men do. He says the souls of horses mirror the souls of men, explaining that if you could understand the soul of a horse, one could understand all horses, but that to understand human beings is probably only an illusion. John Grady also is tutored in the ways of horses by Antonio, the one who helps with the breeding of the mares. Antonio, too, has many ideas about horses and tells John Grady he never lies to the stallion.

The section of the chapter that deals with the breeding of the horses and John Grady's riding of the chestnut stallion leads to the love affair with Alejandra.

John Grady loves to look over the wild mares and pick out the best ones for the shape of their heads, the strength of their legs, and the shape of their hindquarters. He dreamed of producing the best horses for cutting or cattle work, for endurance, and, hopefully, for beauty. What becomes clear from this chapter that highlights the "pretty horses" is that John Grady is exceptionally talented with horses. He rides better than most, as Rawlins has pointed out before, he understands horses, as Rocha observes, and he can very successfully work with horses. Of course, his love of horses is undisputed. He is only 16 years old, but he knows more about the history of horses than most of the other characters in the book, with the exception of Rocha, perhaps. We realize John Grady learned much of this from his grandfather and that during World War II, with other men and his father gone to war, he was, as a young boy, his grandfather's main cowboy.

If the commonality between characters and cultures is a love of horses, the clash of cultures and individuals can also be revealed through the horses. When John Grady says the one thing the wild horses have going for them is that they have not been ridden by the Mexicans, and when he refers to those "damned Mexican ringbits," the reader may wonder if a certain prejudice is being called up. For background on this, an analysis of American western-style riding techniques versus English and Spanish techniques may be helpful.

The "damned ringbit" referred to is a spade bit with a ring that fits around the lower jaw of the horse. It is a very cruel bit by United States western standards. But the experienced, old vaqueros use the ringbit this way: First, they train a young horse with a bosalea, a rope noose that gently fits over the nose but has knots that can put pressure on nerves under the horse's chin and at the side of the mouth. Then, using a second set of reins, they attach the ringbit. When riding the horse, they use the bosalea reins first to correct the horse. If the horse misbehaves, they then use the reins of the ringbit. The ringbit's main flaw is that, when it is used with a heavy hand, it can break the horse's jaw.

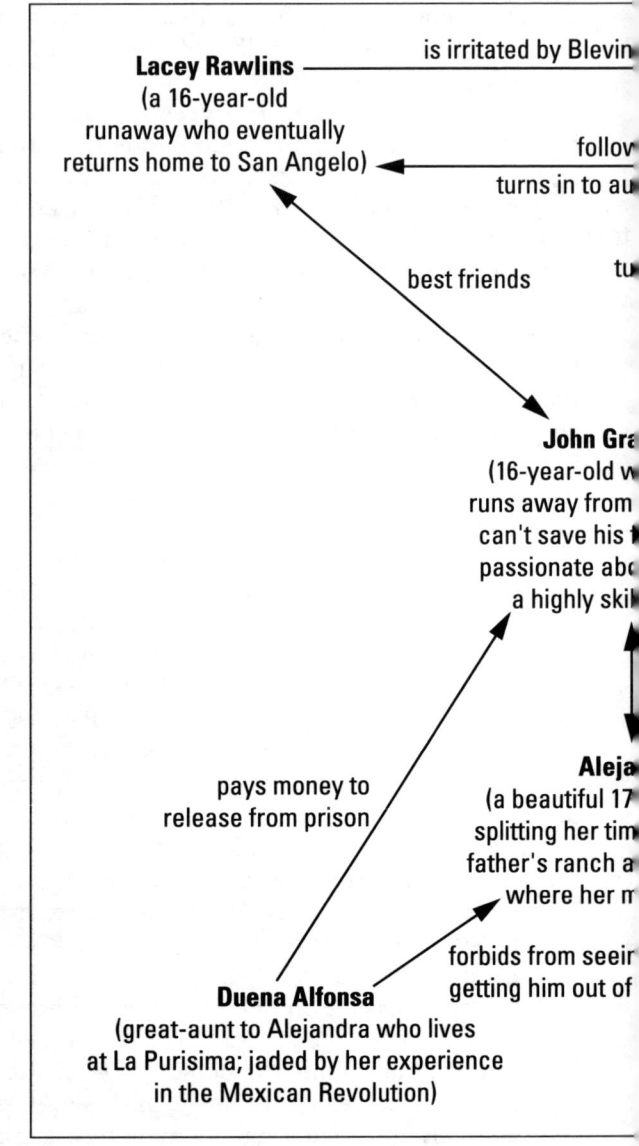

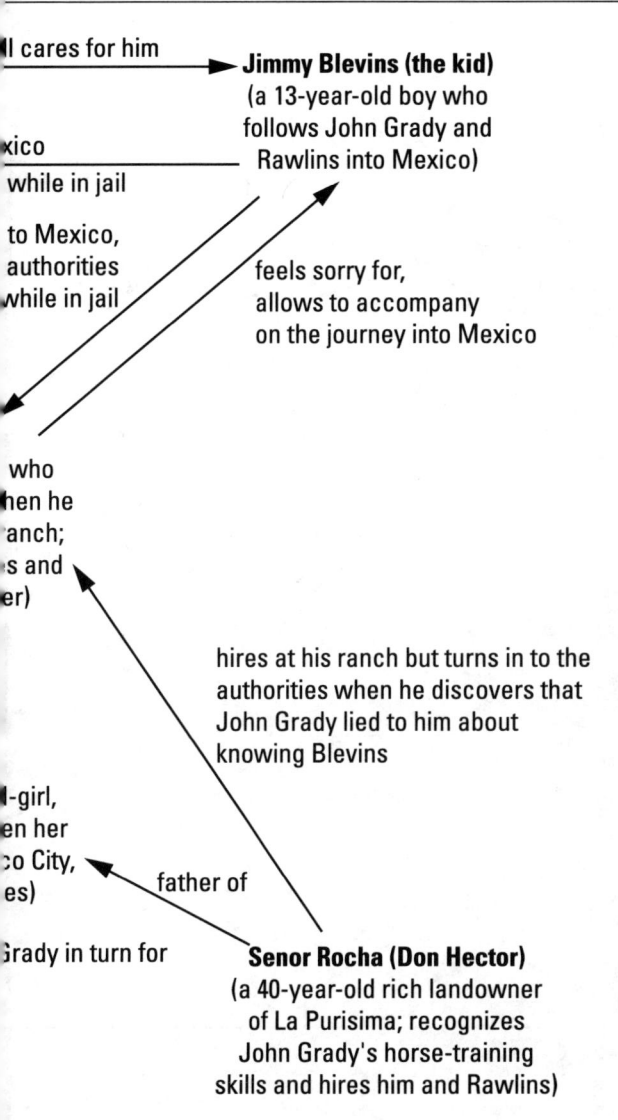

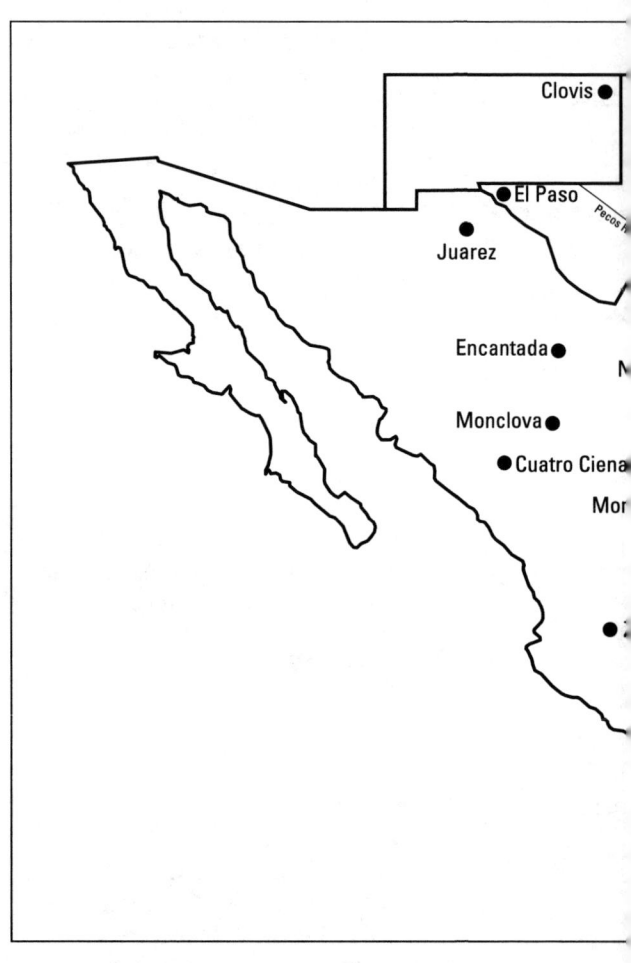

This double-rein method is similar to the double reins used in English riding where the rider uses a tighter double rein to control and signal the horse to change lead or gait. In Western riding, the horse is almost entirely guided with voice commands, leg pressure, and neck reining—where the rein is gently laid on the horse's neck to get it to turn right or left. The well-trained Western horse, even in roping competitions, needs no pulling on the bit. The bit is there only for control if the horse should, because of some unexpected happening, do the wrong thing. Then a little pull gets the animal back on course.

The difference in philosophy is that in Western riding, horse and rider are partners who know the job to be done and work together to do it. The horse takes its cue from the rider and vice versa. In English riding, the rider is more the controller, the one in command. The Spanish riding technique is a combination of these two styles.

The Americans and Mexicans have different training techniques and, perhaps, different philosophies about civilizing the horses. Of these three methods, none is superior or inferior.

The scene in which John Grady and Rocha play billiards, John Grady having told Don Hector that he plays "pool," tells us more about the attitudes of different cultures. Don Hector says that it is a very French idea "that people can be improved in their character by reason." He continues, "Beware, gentle knight. There is no greater monster than reason." He tells John Grady that this idea is a Spanish one, the idea of Quixote. Here it is reason versus feeling, the classic view versus the romantic.

And where does John Grady stand in all of this? McCarthy's work proposes, perhaps, that Americans are neither creatures of reason nor romance, but survivors who risk much and can take actions that appear romantic, but that, all the while, they are committed to their own ideas and ideals; the European tradition is often more deductive and traditional, not as ready to leap to the new, as the American individualist often does. John Grady's work with the horses reveals that he uses reason and control to tame the animals—in the sidelining method. But he has a habit of talking to them and soothing them, and that comes from another idea about nature—that humans can understand horses, can commune with these creatures for better cooperation. This idea is a more romantic one. But it is the goal John Grady is focused on—to get these horses greenbroke—and he uses all his knowledge, his experience, and any technique that he thinks may work. He is eclectic and creative in how he approaches a problem. This is the American way — solve the problem and forget the rulebook or the blueprints. These American attributes come from the whole history of the United States: the American Revolution, the Constitution, the Bill of Rights, the entire struggle for equality, and the development of the frontier. John Grady is definitely a classic American hero, in all his sensibilities.

Another clash of culture is revealed when the great-aunt plays chess with John Grady. He is a worthy opponent and she admires his abilities. But, in conversation, she discusses the role of women in society: "This is another country. Here, a woman's reputation is all she has." She adds, "There is no forgiveness. For women. A man may lose his honor and regain it again. But a woman cannot." John Grady tells her he doesn't think this is fair, indicating the importance that fairness plays in his way of looking at the world. But she dismisses that with a wave of her hand and tells him, "It is a matter of who must say." In other words, power is more important than right. John Grady, Quioxotian in his idealism, understands what she says, but he is not about to change his ideas.

Alejandra is a young woman obviously rebellious like John Grady. She is perhaps even more brash than he is, for it is she who initiates their love affair. But this liberated endeavor is to be allowed by the great-aunt. The great-aunt is determined that Alejandra will not be unhappy as she was in her youth. The reader might also wonder if, because the aunt had an unhappy youth, she does *not* wish to see Alejandra happy in love—something that would only remind her of what she did not have when she was young.

Even though the great-aunt has lived a life of sophistication and ease, teaching in Europe and living, apparently, where she pleases, she has not been able to have a satisfying life. In her shortsightedness, she is determined to mold Alejandra to her likeness, to exercise the control over Alejandra's life that she never had over her own. Unfortunately, she does not have the wisdom to see that happiness is not always found through reason and control, and it certainly is not something the elders can give to the young. In contrast, we see the portrait of John Grady's mother, the American, a generation between the great-aunt and Alejandra, living a liberated life of sorts. Whether she is happy or not we do not know. But she is allowed to make her own way, neither her father nor her husband forbidding or preventing her from making her own choices.

Obviously, the gender issues are not solved in this novel, but, although only a minor theme, these issues do affect John Grady's life. His unusual youth, partly abandoned by his natural mother, and yet well cared for by the old Abuela and Luisa, played a part in shaping his attitudes. The ideas he developed about the position of women in society certainly affect the outcome of his romance at La Purisima. Strangely, Don Hector laments that he is only a father and will not have a say in what Alejandra must do. In Spanish culture, as related to European Mediterranean culture, women have the power in the house and men have total power in the public arena. This separation between public and private life is different from the traditions in the United States. Also, the fact that Mexico is a Catholic country and the United States a Protestant one by tradition, makes the position of women in the two countries quite different. As in all cultures, before women's rights, women manipulate and use what wiles they have to get what they want. The great-aunt is interesting in light of these observations, because she has not been able to really create or direct her own life to her own satisfaction at all. She has been bound by tradition and sent to Europe. Contrast this with John Grady's mother, of whom no one is very fond, but she has led her own life and made her own way in the theatrical world. John Grady, thus, coming from another culture, does not understand that, in the end, Alejandra will not run away with him. He doesn't think that the situation is fair, and, far from his point of view, he thinks it is old-fashioned. But he does not yet comprehend how different his history is from Alejeandra's. He is drawn to Spanish culture, but he is American.

Comparison and contrast of the human relationships and the horses' situations make for interesting insight here. The youths, John Grady and Alejandra, are passionately in love and John Grady is working with the hot-blooded horses. But the adults who are inspecting and observing the youths do not seem to take as much care with their human futures as John Grady does with the horses. When the great-aunt shows him an unusual chess move, he says he'd like to see it again, but of course she will never invite him back; she has only looked him over to certify her preconceived notions of what she wants for Alejandra. The father, who is so careful with his animals, takes no action on his daughter's behalf. There is no education, no training for the young people from the most educated adults. Only the old vaqueros try to impart some wisdom to John Grady. And is anyone trying to impart any helpful knowledge to Alejandra? No wonder their love story is doomed like Romeo and Juliet's.

- **hacendados**   (Spanish) head or owner of the hacienda.
- **barrial**   basin.
- **bolsón**   flat land.
- **Hacienda de Nuestra Senora de la Purisima Concepcion**   (Spanish) Hacienda of Our Lady of the Pure Conception.
- **roan**   a horse that has white hair evenly or sprinkled across its body so that its coat has a mottled appearance; usually red roan or blue roan when mixed with chestnut or black.
- **dun**   a buckskin-colored horse. A true buckskin in decades past was a buttermilk-colored horse with a complete dark dorsal stripe and black points. (Now this sometimes refers to a dun.) The dun color comes from yellow hairs on dark skin. A dun can also have red points.
- **bay**   a brown-colored horse with shades ranging from red and yellow to brown. Points (mane and tail) are black.
- **Paint**   commonly called Indian ponies. These are horses with large irregular patches of black and white or brown and white. Variations are designated pinto, calico, or piebald. Not to be confused with Appaloosa, which is an American breed with distinctive spotting. Roans, duns, bays, and paints are colorings of quarterhorses, although paints now have their own special registry. Originally registered as a color, now as a breed in the United States. In Spain, these horses are called mesquitoes and are special to the king.
- **greenbroke horses**   horses barely rideable and not yet completely trained. "Green," not matured yet.
- **sideline**   a method of tying up the horses to make them stop kicking and bucking (see the preceding Commentary section).

- **Mexican ringbit** a Mexican spade bit with a ring under the mouth; very hard on a horse's mouth.
- **media sangres** (Spanish) medium bloods, or quarterhorses. Horses can be warm bloods or cold bloods as well. Cold bloods are European draft or work horses. Arabians, Barbs, and thoroughbreds are hot bloods.
- **Traveler-Ronda line** Traveler-Ronda was a famous 19th-century Spanish stud, often referred to as a Mexican sand pony; he came from the New Mexico/west Texas region and created one of the Texas foundation lines. He was dun colored.
- **Amansadores** (Spanish) horse trainers, but very special ones who talk softly to wild animals. This is a romantic west.
- **amobs** (Spanish) both.
- **Hay dieciseis caballos en el potrero.** (Spanish) There are sixteen horses in the corral.
- **Podemos amansarlos en cuatro días.** (Spanish) We will be able to break them in four days.
- **bosalea** (Spanish) called a bosal in the United States; a rope noseband used for training.
- **hackamore** a nose-fitting bridle without a bit.
- **manilla** special glove.
- **maguey** the century plant; a large cactus plant with big blue-green leaves or long stems that fan out from the base. A large needle appoints the end. They bloom once in seventeen years, when a huge stalk rises out of the middle of the plant. After the yellow-orange bloom dies, so does the whole plant. Smaller versions are called agave.
- **ixtle** rope made from a type of agave plant.
- **mecates** lead ropes that attach to the horse halter, used in training or leading the horse; here, made of hair.
- **certified peeler** a real bronco buster.
- **sackin** sacking. A method of calming the horse with a piece of cloth. (See the preceding Commentary section for more information.)
- **forefooted** here roping the forefoot and thus tossing it to the ground. Also used in calf roping.
- **grullo** a black horse with white hairs mixed in so that it looks charcoal gray.

- **mesteños** (Spanish) mustangs.
- **potrero** (Spanish) open lot.
- **sulled**   balked, frozen up, cowboy lingo for a horse stopping.
- **remuda** (Spanish) round pen or corral.
- **un ratito** (Spanish) a little while.
- **Como le convenga** (Spanish) Whatever suits you.
- **Criollo**   A warm-blood Spanish stock horse, indispensable to the gaucho, or cowboy, of Argentina. A horse with Barb blood, the Criollo is know to be tough and is usually dun-colored.
- **rechoncha** (Spanish) round or bun-shaped.
- **mescal**   strong Mexican liquor, often known for a worm in the bottom of the bottle.
- **Al contrario** (Spanish) to the contrary.
- **mojado-reverso** (Spanish) rebel, contrary.
- **Es una troca muy fuerte** (Spanish) a very powerful truck.
- **Está un poco cansado de su viaje, pero es muy bonito.** (Spanish) He is a little tired from traveling, but is still very fine.
- **manada** (Spanish) herd.
- **la única cosa** (Spanish) the only thing.
- **Soy commandante de las yeguas, yo y yo solo. Sin la caridad de estas manos no tengas nada. Ni comida ni agua no hijos. Soy yo que traigo las yeguas de las montanas, las yeguas jovenes, las yeguas salvajes y ardientes.**   (Spanish) I am the leader (commander) of the mares, I and I alone. Without the charity of these hands you have nothing. Neither food nor water nor children. I am the one who brings the mares from the mountains, the young mares, the wild and hot-blooded mares.
- **tules**   bulrushes, marsh plants.
- **quinceañera** (Spanish) fifteenth special birthday; coming out party.
- **Te espera.** (Spanish) She is waiting for you.
- **Me quieres?** (Spanish) Do you want me? (Do you love me?)
- **El cuatro. Catorce.** (Spanish) Number four. Fourteen.
- **Ella está aquí. Desde ayer.** (Spanish) She is here. Since yesterday.

- **Quien es?** (Spanish) Who is it?
- **armas** (Spanish) firearm, rifle.
- **En el segundo puesto** (Spanish) in the second stall.

CHAPTER III

Summary

Handcuffed, John Grady Cole and Lacey Rawlins are driven north on their horses for three days. At night, they are manacled to their saddle stirrups and forced to sleep under one blanket this way. They arrive in Encantada, and, while sitting on a bench on the main street, John Grady gestures to two little girls, asking for cigarettes. Rawlins calls him a ladies' man and talks to him for the first time since their capture.

John Grady and Rawlins start to argue. John Grady wants to get their problems out in the open and says they are there because of some lie. Rawlins retorts, "Or some truth." He reminds John Grady that he tried to reason with him (the implication is that he's referring to Alejandra). John Grady says some things aren't reasonable. Grudgingly, Rawlins says he has not quit John Grady. The little girls bring the cigarettes and ask if they are robbers.

John Grady and Rawlins are taken to an adobe prison on the north end of town and find that Blevins is already in the cell. They question him without results. But an old man, also imprisoned in the same cell, tells them that Blevins has killed three men. Blevins says only one died. In order to retrieve his pistol, he returned to Encantada after working for two months. Then he told his captors about John Grady and Rawlins. He can't walk because his feet have been broken.

John Grady dreams of horses that night as he sleeps. In the morning, Rawlins is questioned and asked to strip off his trousers; he is struck on the back of the head. They say he is lying about who he is. He says they are cowboys who have come to work in Mexico. He is asked why the horses have no brands or papers. Then John Grady is questioned. They are accused of having come to Mexico to steal horses. John Grady is told they will be taken to Saltillo.

John Grady tells his interrogators, "There aint but one truth." But they persist in asking questions about Blevins. Back in the cell, John Grady tells Rawlins that he thinks they want a deal to kill Blevins. This upsets Rawlins, but then he gets angry with Blevins and threatens him. John Grady says, "Let it go."

Three days later they are taken from the dark cell into the sunlight and put on a flatbed truck with three guards. They are heading back south to Saltillo. They stop for a break, and the captain has ordered a guard to take Blevins away from the other two. Before he goes, Blevins takes off one boot and gives John Grady his money. The captain and the charro take him into the trees and after "a long time" John Grady and Rawlins hear a pistol shot.

In Saltillo the truck makes various stops before they arrive at the big prison. While waiting in a room, John Grady tells the captain he didn't have to kill Blevins. The captain tells him, "A man does not change his mind." They are locked in a cell and sleep on iron bunks with greasy mattresses. After breakfast in the morning, they are turned loose into a common yard where they have to fight all day. The next day it is the same thing. By the third day, the fights are mostly over, and on the fourth day, Sunday, they buy new clothes with Blevins' money. They share a can of tomato soup they've purchased. Rawlins laments, "All over a goddamned horse." John Grady says it is not about a horse.

A man called Perez has them brought to him and he offers them protection, but no deal is made. The next day, Rawlins is attacked and cut with a knife. John Grady takes him to the gate, and the captors take Rawlins. John Grady goes to see Perez, who, it is rumored, is not a prisoner at all. How much power Perez has no one knows. John Grady arranges to buy a knife. He has another conversation with Perez, which involves a little speech from Perez about the mind of the Anglo. Perez says Americans are godless. There is a prison fight initiated against John Grady by a hired "cuchilero," or slasher (a fighter with a knife). John Grady is badly injured, but he survives because he kills the other man with his knife. John Grady is taken to Perez's room. As his wounds are healing, he thinks of his father and horses. Finally, he is taken to the commandante's office and handed an envelope of money and learns Rawlins is waiting outside for him.

John Grady and Rawlins are let out of the prison and catch a bus to the center of Saltillo. They go to a hotel for food and a room. In their conversations, John Grady makes it clear that he does not want to leave Mexico, because he wants to see Alejandra and he doesn't want to leave the horses. Rawlins is worried for John Grady and talks about Blevins. He still can't believe that Blevins was shot.

They figure that the money John Grady was given in the envelope and their release was procured by Alejandra's great-aunt. They buy new clothes and Rawlins catches a bus for Nuevo Larado. John Grady spends a week seeing surgeons, and, finally, the stitches are removed from his face and belly.

John Grady takes a bus heading north to Monclova.

Commentary

This chapter is the one in which John Grady and Rawlins face their punishment. Here, the two youths spend time in jail, their adventure goes awry, and they are in greater danger than they have ever been in before. Rawlins spends time in a hospital at the prison, and John Grady is seriously wounded. What is the cause of their many problems? John Grady and Rawlins talk about this on their trip north, when they are first captured. Do they face this punishment because of a lie, as John Grady says, or because of the truth, as Rawlins says? It is, of course, a combination of factors, including bad luck. Blevins is a major part of their problems. John Grady and Rawlins helped Blevins because he was so young and without common sense. And he told the authorities who they were. A natural response to Blevins' treatment of John Grady and Rawlins is anger. But Rawlins, who has never defended Blevins and always thought he would bring bad luck, says repeatedly that no one deserves to die like that.

Another obvious reason for their imprisonment is John Grady's lie to Don Hector about coming from Texas alone, just the two of them. Although it is only one lie, it has terrible consequences. The lesson here should not go unheeded.

Rawlins, of course, thinks that the affair with Alejandra is what has landed them in trouble. He tells John Grady that, when the militia came for him in the night, he asked them if Rocha were awake and they laughed at him and said he'd been awake a long time.

The Romeo and Juliet parallel in this novel is quite interesting. Two young lovers have defied their parents, John Grady by running away from home and school and Alejandra by spending lots of time at the ranch. Alejandra is defying all her culture's dictates by having an affair with a poor Americano. She is not only soiling her virtue, she is ignoring her class position. And she is the one who initiates the affair.

Some things are not reasonable, as John Grady tells Rawlins, and indeed the whole history of tragic romances tells us that this is so. Nevertheless, we wish there could be a happy ending for the two lovers.

Finally, the young men are saved from death and imprisonment because of Alejandra and her great-aunt. So, at least, the lovers escape death. But one of the protagonist's friends dies, the one with the least common sense, just as in Shakespeare's *Romeo and Juliet* where Romeo's friend Mercutio dies.

In addition to the Romeo and Juliet motif, we see in *All the Pretty Horses* a *Paradise Lost* theme. First, there is the creation of the characters, by their families and upbringing. Then the two friends take a journey on their horses and find a paradise to live in, jobs they like, great horses to work with, a beautiful setting. They have their first taste of adulthood — no parents making decisions for them. But mistakes are made — helping Blevins, lying about knowing him, and having an affair with the forbidden girl.

John Grady says, "You dont get to go back and pick some time when the trouble started and then lay everthing off on your friend." What John Grady is saying is that luck and fate also play their parts in the way events come to pass. We can clearly see this: If Blevins had just been satisfied to have his horse and not want to go back again to retrieve his pistol, if the great-aunt had wielded her power with more sympathy, if the father had not been so passive about his daughter and a young man he really likes, if the two boys had had papers on their own horses, all would be different.

Instead, they have to endure the horrible prison at Saltillo and learn the most terrible lessons the journey brings them. Rawlins says he never could imagine there was a place like the prison, and both of them are shocked at the inhumane way Blevins is treated. The young American cowboys are finding out about real evil, real terror, and real pain.

In Chapter III, we see much discussion of what a man is or is supposed to be. The daily fighting in the prison yard looks like madness to an outsider. But it is more than survival, it's the way to claim manhood and territory in the prison. Only after the prisoners are severely wounded are they given any help. By this definition, you can only prove your manhood by coming close to death. To be a man is to fight.

Then there is the captain who shoots Blevins. He explains later to John Grady that men talk of honor and justice, but is that what they really want? "A man cannot go back. . . ." "A man does not change his mind." What the captain means is that men cannot look weak or change their minds because it would look bad. Does this mean that what is proclaimed as honor is often only ego or some kind of saving face?

On the other hand, look at the idealism of the young as portrayed by John Grady and sometimes even by Rawlins. When they first meet Blevins and he is asked why they should help him, he says, "Because I'm an American." And they stick by him, partly out of American loyalty, partly because they believe in the Golden Rule. Look where it gets them — in prison. Are the older, more cynical characters people who once were idealists, too? Has life taught them that idealism is inherently false? Remember, the old great-aunt says she was an idealist once herself.

After Rawlins and John Grady arrive in Encantada and are put in the tiny prison cell with Blevins and the old man (who doesn't even know how long he has been there or for what crime), John Grady can still dream of horses when he sleeps. He dreams he runs among the horses, mares, and colts, all of them moving like music, without fear; "They ran in that resonance which is the world itself and which cannot be spoken but only praised." This ability to dream of horses shows that in the middle of his terrible predicament, John Grady is still strongly attached to nature, that his basic spirit is still whole. It isn't just his idealism and ethics that motivate John Grady; it is his whole sense of what is good on the earth that pushes him to make the decisions he does. The way of the land, nature, and the horses have all been his greatest teachers. From them he has learned that one does not abandon the weakest member of the herd, that one lives to ride and run free over the varied terrain, with the winds.

The character of Perez, the man who lives in a special hut on the prison grounds, presents another important lesson for John Grady. Perez says, "You cannot stay in this place and be independent peoples." Later, he talks of the mind of the Anglo and says it is closed in a rare way. He thinks Anglos have an incomplete picture of the world. Perhaps he is saying they don't comprehend cruelty. He also has a unique idea of manhood: "The world wants to know if you have cojones." He cynically says that people who don't have a price die. Later, he says that Americans aren't practical and they think "there are good things and bad things." Are we to see this Perez character as an evil force that John Grady must contend with at the lowest point of his life? Or is Perez the existential survivor who sees that John Grady lives through the terrible stabbing? Some of what Perez says makes some sense, and it may very well be true that "evil is a true thing in Mexico." This may be one of John Grady's lessons. However, it is clear that Perez is also always manipulating his own situation and this makes him a very slippery character, one whose mind is genuinely foreign, not just by nationality, but also temperament.

As an interesting footnote, Rawlins has received over a liter of Mexican blood, and at the end of the chapter it worries him that he might be part Mexican. John Grady teases him about being a half-breed, but has to exclaim, "Hell . . . blood's blood." Neither of them is very happy. They now know the effects of their actions and certain circumstances, but the full power of what has happened to them and their total fall from grace has not totally been understood.

- **selvedge**   also selvage, a woven edge.
- **alameda**   (Spanish) boulevard.
- **sull up**   go sullen or sulky; cowboy lingo.
- **muy amable**   (Spanish) very kind.
- **Son americanos ustedes?**   (Spanish) Are you all Americans?
- **Son ladrones?**   (Spanish) Are you robbers?
- **Sí. Ladrones muy famosos. Bandoleros.**   (Spanish) Yes. Very famous robbers. Bandits.
- **Qué precioso**   (Spanish) How adorable.

- **las esposas** (Spanish) the handcuffs.
- **Cuidado con el bote**   (Spanish) Be careful of the pot.
- **De qué crimen queda acusado el joven?**   (Spanish) What crime is the kid being accused of?
- **El ha matado un hombre?**   (Spanish) He has killed a man?
- **rurales**   (Spanish) country guys.
- **coursed**   ran.
- **Quita las esposas**   (Spanish) Take the handcuffs off.
- **Somos vaqueros**   (Spanish) We are cowboys.
- **marca**   (Spanish) brand.
- **factura**   (Spanish) registered papers.
- **cazador**   (Spanish) hunter.
- **charro**   (Spanish) Mexican cowboy; picturesque.
- **Sólo el chico**   (Spanish) only the boy.
- **Están esperando.**   (Spanish) They are waiting.
- **quinta**   (Spanish) country house.
- **paseos**   (Spanish) strolls, walks.
- **Se llama la periquera.**   (Spanish) I am called the parakeet (bird).
- **santo**   (Spanish) saints' day.
- **pozole**   (Spanish) cornmeal mush.
- **gabachos**   (Spanish) derogatory for French person; derived from "gabacha," meaning "apron."
- **bolillos**   (Spanish) drumsticks; here, an insulting term.
- **satrap**   petty tyrant.
- **alcaide**   (Spanish) jailer or guard.
- **cuchillero**   (Spanish) a brawler or person clever with a knife.
- **Quisiera hablar con el señor Peréz.**   (Spanish) I would like to talk with Sr. Perez.
- **Con respecto de que?**   (Spanish) With respect to what?
- **Con respecto de mi cuate**   (Spanish) In regard to my buddy.
- **Me toma el pelo.**   (Spanish) He/she fools me (pulls my hair).

- **castellano** (Spanish) Spanish.
- **previas** (Spanish) preliminary hearing.
- **cojones** (Spanish) balls, testicles.
- **Quiero comprar una trucha.** (Spanish) I would like to buy a knife.
- **Cúanto dinero tienes?** (Spanish) How much money do you have?
- **cuarenta Y cinco pesos** (Spanish) forty-five pesos.
- **Bueno. La tendre esta tarde.** (Spanish) Good. I will have it this afternoon.
- **punche** (Spanish) low class, potent, homegrown tobacco.
- **esclarajo** (Spanish) lighter.
- **Nó tienes visitantes?** (Spanish) Don't you have any visitors?
- **Hay un cordón.** (Spanish) There is a cord.
- **tamalera** (Spanish) seller of tamales.
- **El padrote quiere ayudarle.** (Spanish) The patron wants to help you.
- **Dame el refresco. Nada más.** (Spanish) Give me a pop. Nothing more.
- **Mejor que nunca** (Spanish) Better than ever.
- **Quién és usted?** (Spanish) Who are you?
- **Sus prendas** (Spanish) Your clothes.
- **Dónde está mi compadre?** (Spanish) Where is my friend?

CHAPTER IV

Summary

From Saltillo, John Grady catches rides north on a truck with farm workers whose goodwill he appreciates. They arrive in Monclova at midnight. He sleeps on a bench and the next day has a breakfast of coffee and pan dulce before catching two more rides. He bathes in an irrigation ditch and starts to walk toward Cuatro Cienagas. Everyone speaks to John Grady as they pass, and, in the evening, workers in a camp invite him to supper. Through a series of rides, he makes his way beyond Nadadores, out of La Madrid, and into La Vega. After buying a Coke in a small store, he starts walking toward La Purisima, and after dark he knocks on the manager's door, only to find that Sr. Rocha and Alejandra are in Mexico City. Antonio gives John Grady his and Rawlins' belongings.

John Grady sleeps in his old room in the barn, and, in the morning at breakfast, he is told that Alejandra's great-aunt has invited him to see her that evening at ten o'clock. He asks if he can ride the horse, and he takes the stallion out for the day, riding across the lands of the beautiful hacienda. He thinks of Alejandra and Blevins. At one point, he passes a dead colt being devoured by buzzards. Later, he comes upon an abandoned cabin. He picks an apple, but it is too green to eat and the cattle have eaten all the ripened apples from the ground. The stallion is nervous in the old cabin and, on the ride home, is afraid of its own shadow.

He has a cigarette with the vaqueros who ask him about Rawlins, whom they miss. They tell John Grady the news, but nothing of the Rocha family. He goes to the kitchen and waits to see the old señorita. Alejandra's great-aunt tells John Grady he has been a great disappointment to Sr. Rocha and a great expense to her. He replies, "I've been some inconvenienced myself." John Grady is angry that he didn't have the opportunity to tell his side of the story. She says that the Rocha family had John Grady investigated, and they found he lied twice. She confirms what he had suspected — that Alejandra promised never to see him again if the aunt paid for him to be released. They argue about the recent events, and then the great-aunt tells John Grady more of her life's story, about the Mexican Revolution and the Maderos. She talks about her father and his philosophy. She recounts the poverty in Mexico when she was young. She explains how Gustavo Madero helped her face her handicap after the shooting accident and how he was brutally treated — burned and shot after his arrest. She relates how Francisco Madero was also shot and how the family went into exile. She talks about the bonds of grief, about how she stayed in Europe and taught school in London until after her father's death. Now she visits his grave near the house and talks to him. John Grady asks again to be able to make his case, and she tells him she knows his case.

The next morning John Grady tells his friends goodbye and picks out the horse he calls "Rawlins' grullo." At noon, near farmland, he stops to have his lunch given to him at the hacienda, and he shares it with some children who want to know his story. So he tells them of Rawlins and Blevins and Alejandra. An older girl tells him he is forgetting that he is poor and the family is rich. She says he should appeal to the "grandmother," meaning the oldest female member of his intended's family. When he tells them that is not possible, they suggest a medicine woman. Finally, they tell him to pray.

John Grady rides to Torreon and phones Alejandra in Mexico City. Finally, she agrees to meet him in Zacatecas on her way to the hacienda. She will travel by train. He stables the grullo and catches a train and arrives in Zacatecas in the late afternoon. He gets a room in the Reina Cristina Hotel and walks around the old city. Alejandra's train is late and he almost doesn't recognize her in a blue dress and hat. She tells him he is thin. They walk and have dinner in a public place where the men stare at her. He tells her everything. Alejandra does not understand John Grady, or men in general, and says, "What are men?" Alejandra tells him that she told her father of their affair. "How could you tell him?" John Grady responds. Alejandra cries. She believes that her father did not kill John Grady in the mountains when the greyhounds came into the camp because he was afraid Alejandra would commit suicide if he did.

In the hotel room, John Grady asks Alejandra to go away with him. In the morning, she tells him she had a dream some time ago in which she saw him dead and she made a promise for his life. She takes him to the plaza where her grandfather died in 1914, serving under one of the Maderos. They go to the hotel room and make love, and she tells him she cannot go with him. He takes her to the train, where they part for the last time. He gets drunk, and in the morning he does not know where he is. He hitchhikes back to Torreon. He buys shells for his pistol and rides into the countryside. That night, he camps without a fire and listens to his horse grazing. He thinks about the pain of the world. Five days later, John Grady comes to a crossroads and decides to go the other way to La Encantada. "I aint leavin my horse down here."

He captures the captain who shot Blevins, and they ride to the hacienda where the horses are. After some fighting and the passive help of a charro, he does retrieve his horses, but eventually he must leave the grullo behind, because it is not strong enough for the trip. But he is able to travel with Redbo, Junior, and Blevins' big bay. John Grady has rigged a pistol to shoot after he and the horses are farther away, and it does, leading their followers off the trail. He keeps the captain as a hostage and doctors himself by putting a fire-heated pistol into his wounds to cauterize them. The captain says he can go no father, but John Grady helps him by pulling his shoulder back into place. He awakens to three men of the country standing over him. They take the keys and the captain, but they give John Grady a blanket. He never sees them again. He rides all day, headed north, killing a small doe for food.

John Grady crosses the river west of Langtry, undressed with his boots stowed, as he had entered Mexico in "that long ago," as McCarthy notes. In Texas, naked, he sits on his horse and looks at the pale landscape and knows his father is dead in that country. He weeps. John Grady knows this only by intuition, and he is right. In the town of Langtry, he finds out it is Thanksgiving Day. He rides the border country for days, trying to find the owner of the big bay. Then, just before Christmas, three men try to go to court to get the horse. He tells his story to the judge, who thinks kindly of John Grady and sends him on his way. After hearing a reverend named Jimmy Blevins on the radio, he goes to Del Rio to meet the man. The preacher and his wife feed John Grady and tell him the horse is not theirs. They have no memory of anyone fitting Blevins' description. The minister tells him how he came to be a radio personality. John Grady never finds the owner of the horse, and, finally, the first week of March, he is back in San Angelo.

He goes to Rawlins' house and whistles to get Rawlins' attention. John Grady returns Rawlins' horse, Junior, to his friend. When Rawlins asks John Grady what he's going to do next, John Grady says he's going to head out. Rawlins points out that it's still "good country," and John Grady says, "Yeah. I know it is. But it aint my country." Before John Grady rides away, he goes to the funeral of Abuela. He stands across the road, and, after all the mourners leave, he walks the cemetery where he knows most of the Spanish names. He rides west, leading his second horse. Some camped Indians watch him, without any reaction.

Commentary

The final chapter is the unraveling and unwinding of all that has come before. It begins with the outcast theme, as John Grady, injured but healing, makes his way back to La Purisima. It contains the greatest disillusionment of the novel, when Alejandra rejects John Grady and leaves him forever. And it continues to answer the cause and effect questions — this most clearly seen in the meeting between John Grady and Alejandra's great-aunt.

John Grady is portrayed as the wanderer, wandering with some purpose until the very last page when he sets out with Redbo and the big bay to become only a silhouette on the horizon. Until this moment, he has ridden with purpose — to try to find Alejandra, to retrieve his horses, to find the owner of the big bay. But at the end of the novel, he joins those who wander forever.

Mexico has let down John Grady. It is a land of cruelties he had not imagined when he first came upon its beauty. The great-aunt is rigid in her adherence to reason. She has no sympathy for the young, the idealist (even if she thinks she once was one herself), the romantic. And Alejandra is too educated and tied to her society to run away with John Grady. She even refers to herself as a whore because of the affair she had with John Grady, clearly unable to reconcile the passion she felt toward John Grady with the role she has been groomed to play.

So all of John Grady's Mexican adventures have resulted in him being an outcast again. Was it not enough that John Grady was cast out from his own family ranch after his grandfather's death? Now he has to endure leaving another beloved landscape. He takes the stallion on a day's ride across the property, just as he had taken a last ride with Redbo on the Texas ranch. But here, in Chapter IV, the images are even more onerous: the dead colt being eaten by buzzards, the cabin that has some kind of spooky spirit that bothers the horse ("There was a strange air to the place. As of some site where life had not succeeded."). Is John Grady's destiny to fail as those before him failed?

But although sadness and loss pervade this chapter, goodwill is also a strong force We see that goodwill in the children who share lunch with John Grady and try to advise him on how to win Alejandra back; in the country peasants who take the captain away from John Grady but leave John Grady with his horses and even give him a blanket, taking pity on his plight and blessing him with their kindness; in the many people who feed John Grady; in the judge who believes him and lets him keep the bay horse; and in the Reverend Jimmy Blevins and his wife, who feed him a huge meal. These people, all of whom are strangers, offer advice and help to John Grady.

The person from whom John Grady learns the most is the judge. Forthcoming with wisdom and advice, he tells John Grady that he is being too hard on himself. The judge points out that the prisoner John Grady killed was not a good person and reminds him that the captain was not a peace officer at all. The judge is trying to teach John Grady that there really are, after all, good men and bad men in this world, and we must be able to distinguish between the two.

Disillusion is a major theme in Chapter IV. Rawlins is going home, but neither he nor John Grady is happy. When Alejandra leaves John Grady in Zacatecas, there is more than disillusion; there is a sense of foreboding and doom. Thus, when John Grady makes it back to San Angelo with the three American horses, it is a testament to his strength of will. Sheer willpower brings John Grady back to Texas to his friend Rawlins, whom he has never wanted to let down. One of John Grady's best qualities is loyalty, and he demonstrates this to the end. John Grady also demonstrates his honesty; it is because he believes in honesty and truth that he travels for three months in the border region searching for the original owner of Blevins' big bay. The one inconsistency in John Grady's character is the lie he tells to Rocha when he says he doesn't know Blevins. The fact that such an honest and honorable person could be lowered to this level serves as a warning to all of us of what can happen if we ignore our sense of right and wrong.

In the end, having traveled and learned lessons he could not have anticipated, John Grady is alone to face the death and funeral of Abuela, the old grandmother who raised him. The novel comes full circle, from the grandfather's death in the beginning to the death of his Mexican caretaker. And both the ranches, Texan and Mexican, offer no future for John Grady. So he sets out to travel west, to New Mexico, perhaps in search of another ranch — a bittersweet ending to a wonderful adventure.

The last scene of *All the Pretty Horses*, in which John Grady rides into the red sunset, is what can be referred to as western existentialism. The myth of the cowboy in the west is present, but the image is demythologized. To visualize the scene is to see that classic scene from *Gone with the Wind* of the riders and stragglers walking across the hill in silhouette against the sky. Scarlett does return to Tara (which is similar to the Latin word "terra," meaning earth, signifying her connection to her family's land) and she does survive, but she loses her Rhett. John Grady loses Alejandra, so there is a parallel there as well. Scarlett's great passion is the land and running the plantation to make money so she will never starve again. John Grady's passion is horses and wanting to have a ranch. Because the land is often so barren in the western border region, few admit to loving that land the way Scarlett loved her beautiful Tara, but in *Cities of the Plain*, John Grady and another cowboy have a discussion in which they admit they find this land very satisfying. Yet it is the work and love of horses, and ranching with them, that drives John Grady. He loves his friends with great loyalty, just as Scarlett cares for her family, but essentially it is the landscape they are both tied to, even if the connections to that landscape have differing sources. John Grady cannot be attached to his family ranch, because it is irretrievably lost, so he moves on in the quest for "the" ranch.

The silhouette on the horizon is a modern image, perhaps first used in the movie *Gone with the Wind*, and now come to represent the modern dilemma of displaced people. The other movie that has used that image with great power is Ingmar Bergman's *The Seventh Seal*, in which the characters are dancing in silhouette at the end, after death has taken them all, except for the artist, wife, and baby. Strong parallels exist between this movie and *All the Pretty Horses*: the longing for home, and the knight who has been on an arduous quest, only to return and have to play chess with Death on a regular basis. John Grady's quest is not over at the end of *All the Pretty Horses* and he will continue to search for a home, but he has certainly been playing chess with Death. He survives for now, but when will he be checkmated?

John Grady — a lover of horses, passionate, rash, strong, stubborn, and, for now, a survivor — joins a long line of memorable characters.

McCarthy adds a great touch to the final scene, just before we see the last of John Grady. He passes some Indians camped on the western plains.

> The indians stood watching him. He could see that none of them spoke among themselves or commented on his riding there nor did they raise a hand in greeting or call out to him. They had no curiosity about him at all. As if they knew all that they needed to know. They stood and watched him pass and watched him vanish upon that landscape solely because he was passing. Solely because he would vanish.

The key phrases here are "he was passing" and "he would vanish." What McCarthy is concluding is that all of us are just passing along, both on and in the landscape, and we *all* will vanish. The point of the novel is not the myth, or the heroics, or even the survival. Perhaps, like the knight of faith, John Grady does go out each day to fend off evil and try to do good. But in the end he is just passing by.

The final words of the novel — ". . . horse and rider and horse passed on and their long shadows passed in tandem like the shadow of a single being. Passed and paled into the darkening land, the world to come. . . ." — remind us of Katherine Anne Porter's story of death, "Pale Horse, Pale Rider." The horse and rider are becoming pale or transparent, like a photo dissolving. The land is "darkening," signaling not just the end of the day, but the end of the dreams, the end of the old way of life, and, ultimately, death.

We know the novel has circled back to San Angelo from the grandfather's funeral to Abuela's funeral. Will John Grady be like all the great uncles who never died in bed or on their own ranch? Or will he find a ranch and turn out more like the man he was named after? A certain sense of doom lingers here at the end. The reader can choose to leave the story with a sense of hope, because of John Grady's ability to survive. Or the reader can take the signs of fading and darkness to mean John Grady is destined to fade into darkness as well.

- **De dónde viene?**   (Spanish) Where are you from?
- **Tejas. Y dónde va?**   (Spanish) Texas. And where are you going?

- **El va a ver a su novia.** (Spanish) He is going to see his girlfriend.
- **pan dulce** (Spanish) sweet bread.
- **Quién está en las casa?** (Spanish) Who is in the house?
- **Se fue él y la hija a Mexico. Por avión.** (Spanish) He and the young girl fled to Mexico City. By airplane.
- **Cuándo regresa?** (Spanish) When does he return?
- **Quién sabe?** (Spanish) Who knows?
- **Tus cosas quedan aqui.** (Spanish) Your things are here.
- **Sí. Tu pistola. Todas tus cosas. Y las de tu compadre.** (Spanish) Yes. Your pistol. All your things. And those of your friend.
- **Yo no se nada, joven.** (Spanish) I know nothing, young one.
- **Entiendo** (Spanish) I understand.
- **En serio** (Spanish) It is serious.
- **Está bien. Puedo dormir en lad cuadra?** (Spanish) It is okay. May I sleep in the stable?
- **Sí. Si no me lo digas.** (Spanish) Yes. If you don't tell me.
- **Cómo están las yeguas?** (Spanish) How are the mares?
- **mochila** (Spanish) pack or knapsack.
- **Puedes esperar aquí. Se levantará pronto.** (Spanish) You can wait here. She will get up soon.
- **Quisiera un caballo.** (Spanish) I would like a horse.
- **Sí. Por el día, no más.** (Spanish) Yes. For the day, no more.
- **Tienes tu caballo. Espérate un momento. Siéntate.** (Spanish) You may have the horse. Wait a moment. Sit.
- **Ándale pues** (Spanish) Well, let's go.
- **vigas** (Spanish) beams.
- **tacked and quartered** a riding technique that makes the horse move with a special gait so that it moves forward, but with its body at an angle.
- **Estás bienvenido aquí.** (Spanish) You are welcome here.
- **Ya comiste?** (Spanish) Have you eaten?
- **adobada sauce** marinated sauce.
- **Siéntate. Hay tiempo.** (Spanish) Sit. There is time.

- **Está en las sala.** (Spanish) She is in the parlor.
- **gachupines**   (Spanish) lower-class Mexicans whose speech has a twang.
- **soldadera**   (Spanish) female soldier.
- **cara y cruz**   (Spanish) heads or tails.
- **Teníamos compradrazgo con su familia.**   (Spanish) We had a good empathy with their family.
- **quinceañera**   (Spanish) coming out party at age fifteen.
- **mozo**   (Spanish) young servant.
- **Ojo Parado**   (Spanish) Glass Eye.
- **abrazo**   (Spanish) embrace.
- **Puede vivir con nosotros**   (Spanish) You can live with us.
- **Es bonita, su novia?**   (Spanish) She is beautiful, your intended?
- **De acuerdo**   (Spanish) Of course, or agreed.
- **Que ofensa le dio a la abuelita?**   (Spanish) What offense did you give the grandmother?
- **Es una historia larga**   (Spanish) It is a long story.
- **curandera**   (Spanish) medicine woman; folk doctor who cures; wise old woman.
- **Puede dejarlo atrás**   (Spanish) You can put it back.
- **afuera**   (Spanish) outside.
- **Por dónde?**   (Spanish) Where?
- **Por aquí?**   (Spanish) Through here?
- **Hice una manda**   (Spanish) I have made a promise.
- **Lloraba to madre. Con más razón tu puta.**   (Spanish) Your mother was crying. With more reason than your whore.
- **callejones**   (Spanish) alleys.
- **melcocchas and charamuscas**   (Spanish) taffy(s) and candy twists.
- **alcatraz**   shape to stuff things in.
- **Quién fue el Pensador Mexicano?**   (Spanish) Who was this Mexican thinker?
- **Cierra la puerta**   (Spanish) Close the door.

- **criada** (Spanish) maid.
- **Mande?** (Spanish) Come again? What?
- **Ya estás, viejo? Sí, cómo no. Ven aqui.** (Spanish) You are already old? Yes, of course. Come here.
- **No lo mire a él. Te lo digo yo. Ándale.** (Spanish) Don't look at him. I tell you. Go forward.
- **quiero mi caballo** (Spanish) I want my horse.
- **Tú. Dónde están los otros caballos.** (Spanish) You. Where are the other horses.
- **Tenemos un preso** (Spanish) I have a prisoner.
- **Un ladrón** (Spanish) A thief.
- **Tenemos que ver un caballo** (Spanish) We have to see a horse.
- **Qúe pasó, hombre?** (Spanish) What happened, man?
- **Quién está contigo?** (Spanish) Who is with you?
- **No tire el caballo** (Spanish) Don't shoot the horse.
- **No me mate** (Spanish) Don't kill me.
- **Pásale. Nadie le va a molestar.** (Spanish) Pass on. No one will hurt you.
- **Está loco** (Spanish) You are crazy.
- **Tiene razón** (Spanish) I have my reasons.
- **carabinero** (Spanish) rifleman.
- **Quítese su camisa** (Spanish) Take off your shirt.
- **No tiene otra salida** (Spanish) No other way out.
- **Está compuesto?** (Spanish) Is it set?
- **Deme las llaves** (Spanish) Give me the keys.
- **Cuáles de los caballos son suyos?** (Spanish) Which of the horses are yours?
- **Todos son míos.** (Spanish) They are all mine.
- **Donde está su serape?** (Spanish) Where is your blanket?
- **No tengo.** (Spanish) I have none.

- **veronica** (Spanish) pass with the cape; a special movement in bullfights. Veronica refers to how the cape is held, in the manner of St. Veronica as she wiped Christ's brow. A very graceful movement in the bullfight.
- **Hombres del país** (Spanish) Men of the country.
- **huevos revueltos** (Spanish) scrambled eggs.
- **canela** (Spanish) cinnamon.
- **comal** (Spanish) a hot iron or grill used over an open fire.
- **lay hands on** in Christianity, a way of passing on the power of the Holy Spirit. Sometimes used by clergy, like Reverend Blevins, for healing purposes.
- **crystal set** an old kind of radio, with an earphone for hearing. The crystal picked up the sounds.

CRITICAL ESSAY

THE HORSES OF *ALL THE PRETTY HORSES* AND THE AMERICAN DREAM

The horses in *All the Pretty Horses* play a critical role, which is why specific horses are listed as characters in the front of these notes. The horses are more than a means of transportation for John Grady and Rawlins; they are friends. For example, when John Grady Cole finds Redbo in a stable after his long incarceration and travels on the grullo, Redbo whinnies, or calls to him in a touching reunion. The novel is centered around the horses: catching them, riding them, breeding them, rescuing them, admiring them, talking about them, philosophizing about them. They are the core, the soul, of the novel.

But the horses mean more to John Grady and Rawlins not just because they've formed bonds with them. Horses carry with them centuries of meaning, tied to legend and myth, romance and battle. When McCarthy uses the word grail in the first chapter of the book, we connect the horses to the romance of adventure that goes back in western culture to the crusades. Ever since that medieval period when, according to legend, women gave men their scarves and waved them off to romantic undertakings, men have gone, often on their horses, to fight wars. Here, in this book, are all the same ingredients. Except instead of being the glorious legend of times past, this story is skewed, like light shining through a prism. What we see on the other side isn't the same as what came before. We have no happy ending, no glorious victory with love awaiting the victors. Not that there were, necessarily, happy endings during earlier historic times, but our notions of romance make us believe there were. McCarthy is a realistic mythmaker. His ending is not happy, but it is not totally tragic either. This is why it can be called "western existentialism." John Grady's father has come back from war injured and altered for the worse. The Mexican Revolution that affects so much of what happens in Mexico is 40-year-old history, and it stays with those who lived through it, haunting them and affecting their lives decades later. Yet romance and adventure still reverberate in the undertaking of the two young men when they take their horses and head south. The common thread is the horses.

The horses represent more than just themselves, and they also are the center axis around which the novel revolves. The horses connect all the characters. They connect John Grady to his parents, to his grandfather, to his other ancestors. Even Rawlins says he had seen his father rattle a few times on a horse, indicating that he was a cowpuncher, too, and most likely broke a few horses as Rawlins did. Horses connect the men and women, not just John Grady and Alejandra, but his parents. His father tells him that the two (his parents) had in common a great love of horses, and they were mistaken in thinking that was enough. The horses connect John Grady and Don Hector, owner of the hacienda, who can spend hours talking of the merits of individual horses. The two of them have even read some of the same horse books. The horses tie John Grady, Rawlins, and Blevins together, even after Blevins' death, as John Grady tries to find the rightful owner of Blevins' big bay horse. The horses connect all the cowboys and vaqueros. They connect the old men and the young, the Mexicans and the Americans.

Perhaps most importantly, the horses connect the present to the past. The imagined scenes John Grady sees on his lone rides on the prairie are of the Comanches in the past on their ponies.

Horses connect the events of this era back to the conquistadors who brought the horses back to America, after the indigenous horses of America had long been extinct.

The horses are also the connection to work — working the cattle on ranches and play, riding to hunt or just for pleasure. In short, the horses are connected to all the enterprises of the characters. This includes transportation. Horses still had an important function in 1949, often still used in farming. In the western half of the country, kids still went to school on their ponies, and in the blizzard of 1949, after weeks of being snowed in, fathers finally got to town by horseback. John Grady and Rawlins are too poor to own a car in this novel. In the fifty years since the novel takes place, this has all reversed, so that everyone has a car, many equipped to get through heavy snow, and only the rich can afford horses. The horse, thus, has become a creature for pleasure, and has lost its work function.

When John Grady was a child, an oil painting of horses hung above the sideboard in the formal dining room of the ranch house. Six wild-eyed horses were breaking through a pole corral with manes flying. The horses had Andalusian and Barb features, and as John Grady grew, he analyzed them and saw that they had good cutting horse hindquarters. But something seemed askew because the heads, bodies, and legs of the horses did not fit as he'd seen them in real horses. He finally asked his grandfather what kind of horses these were. His grandfather tells him they are "picturebook horses." But we learn when John Grady is breeding wild mares with Rocha's chestnut stallion from Kentucky that these are the kind of horses Rocha and the young American cowboy now dreamed of producing.

So the horses are also the link between art and real life. First, an artist imagined these horses, quickly dismissed between bites of food by the grandfather, but remembered by John Grady. They impress John Grady's mind's eye and give him an idea that he later actually starts to carry out. A connection exists between idea, art, and even the forms of the domesticated horses.

A major energy the horses bring to the novel is to connect human beings to nature. The horses are part of the fabulous landscape scenes described here, in the desert southwest as well as the varied vegetation of Mexico, and often with magnificent mountains as a backdrop. But the horses do more than take the characters into the wilderness, into areas of great earthly beauty. They also help them leave, or escape, areas of harshness and danger.

It is to the nature of the horses themselves that many of the characters are drawn. After centuries of training and domestication of horses by men, we still cannot truly understand them and are often surprised by their behavior. John Grady reminds Rawlins, when he is sacking out the first wild Mexican mustang, that he does not know how a horse thinks. But John Grady is praised by Don Hector for understanding horses and, indeed, he does have the skills and instincts to work wonders with the horses. This is because John Grady has a spiritual connection to the horses, and he totally accepts them in all their power. To be in a pasture with a great stallion and several bands of mares and be accepted in their circle is an awesome experience. There is no explanation for why horses, even penned, accept some people and not others. And the horses do accept John Grady. This spiritual connection may be why John Grady can ride that wild chestnut stallion in the breeding season, a feat few would attempt. John Grady is a real cowboy who is capable of amazing feats with horses. This can be contrasted to the current rodeo, which some defend as the last place where people can exhibit their prowess with horses, cattle, and ropes. It is unfortunate that a needed skill has now developed into a sport only. Larry McMurtry has criticized this in *Rodeo*, "the West. . . . My grip about rodeo, as publicly promoted, is that it wants both the lie and the truth: to be both the Wild West, and yet steeped in family values." He, like McCarthy, uses social protest in his novels.

In another quote from McMurtry, we get at the problem of the romance and myths even more. "I thought *Lonesome Dove* was antimythic. Malory may have felt the same way about the Morte D'Arthur. Readers suck so hard at the old myths, that they turn stones into sour grapes." It is this degradation of the myth, of cowboys and horse, that McCarthy is trying to deal with and elevate in *All the Pretty Horses*. He is portraying the dreams and legends as we still imagine, but he is also casting a realistic eye on all of it.

Horses do carry with them the images of romance, of time long past. The romance endures, which is partly why horses have become so popular again. But the social protest of authors like

McCarthy warns us that we are not able to relive the past. We, and the horses, must exist in a landscape that is dwindling in size and changing in use.

So the images that the pretty horses call up are not all positive and romantic. Aside from commercialization in rodeos, other dark sides to pretty horses do exist. One vaquero tells John Grady that to see the soul of a horse is a terrible thing. It is not just power and beauty that horses call up, but fear and fear of death even. Another old vaquero tells John Grady that horses love war. The idea that horses have a cruel side is not developed by McCarthy, but here the old man seems to be saying that horses like to strive, compete, and battle. Even if horses are essentially creatures of flight, who run from danger, they will fight for territory and also when trapped. This death theme of horses adds to the John Grady myth.

We are enamored, because he is young, he is very bright, he is on a quest. He is a cowboy. What is the romance of the cowboy in American culture? It is the romance the idealist has always elicited. The man of action still thrills—maybe especially because of the age of anxiety we live in. Romantic figures can call up something timeless, something so thrilling we can't avoid it. The horses are an integral part of this romance. They are huge domesticated animals that have accompanied mankind on our adventures and travels for centuries. Almost every culture of the world has prized and used them — with the exception of some island societies, perhaps. They are beautiful creatures, which is why they lend themselves to more pretty romance than camels, for example. Horses are a connection to the most awesome, powerful, and beautiful parts of nature. When a man can train and ride a great horse, he partakes of that power and beauty that so often eludes us. Then nature is not quite so overpowering or frightening. If we can survive the horse gallop, we can do anything.

Whatever the negatives, it is hard to not return to the romance. But there are also the realists, and Rawlins is the main one in the novel, who try to get John Grady, as well as the reader, back to earth. Rawlins had said in Chapter I, "A good lookin horse is like a good lookin woman. . . . They're always more trouble than what they're worth." This homespun philosophy gives the book and John Grady the needed realistic dialogue. But in the end, John Grady risks his life again to bring the horses home to America.

They are not just transportation, not just animals. They are John Grady's lifeblood. And much more.

So the cowboy has a special masculine aura, partly the aura all great athletes have, going back to the Greeks, but a more special one because the aura of the horse is inextricably bound up with the cowboy's aura. As many have noted, rider and horse are one being, not two. This masculinity is so strong that the cowboy need not say much at all. The power of the horse communicates for him, with him. The vision of him on his horse is enough. This is not sexuality. It is skill, profound connection to the earth and sky. It is horse, pretty horse. The pretty horses are legend, myth, romance, nature, and spirituality; and John Grady, on his quest, supposedly to find a ranch, or home, throws himself into all of that. This is why one of the meanings for "pretty horses" must be the American Dream.

No American, or perhaps now even citizen of the world, can escape that. The New World was conquered, if that is the word we must use, by adventurers in search of gold. They took great risks in their searches and not all of them came for gold. The Jesuit and Franciscan monks walked so far in the desert, sometimes totally alone for dreams, of course. Dreams of serving God. Dreams of finding something new. Dreams of a better life. And those of us who have come after are forever in awe of the risks they all took, the suffering they endured. This is why to read *All the Pretty Horses* is to love not only the book and the story, but John Grady and the young characters as well. We admire them, we are frightened for them, we envy them, we do romanticize them. And is that so terrible? These young adventurers are surely the stuff dreams are made of. Adults steeped in reason, just like the adults in the novel, are way too hard on John Grady; "He is only sixteen-years-old." John Grady is a realist as well as ideal character, for his time and place. But he also is larger than life, mythic at sixteen. Definitely a cowboy. Definitely a lover of horses.

John Grady, on his horse, is the bearer of a whole history, how perhaps a tragic one. Are the "pretty horses" dying? Do the horse and rider, who have achieved so much, also risk losing everything? At the end of *All the Pretty Horses*, they are still alive, their shadows a single being, where they "passed and paled into the darkening land, the world to come." This may be the rider of pale horse, pale rider, linked to death. But it may also be the modern rider, still moving, or dancing, with the forces of existence. In any case, one cannot separate the pretty horses from the rider, or from the dreams.

REVIEW QUESTIONS AND ESSAY TOPICS

(1) Compare one of the camping scenes with Rawlins and John Grady with a camping scene from Hemingway (for example, *The Sun Also Rises* or one of the Nick Adams stories).

(2) Compare and contrast the breaking of the horses in Chapter II with Faulkner's "Spotted Horses."

(3) What is the significance of the picture of the horses in the Grady formal dining room, the horses his grandfather called "picturebook"?

(4) What is the significance of the antiques in the Grady ranch house? Compare and contrast these antiques to the ones at La Purisima.

(5) What is the significance of John Grady's mother pursuing an acting career? Why does she never have a name?

(6) When John Grady says goodbye to his girlfriend, Mary Catherine, in Texas, he feels he has "stepped out of the glass forever." When Alejandra tells him she cannot go with him, his life feels that it will lead nowhere at all. Compare and contrast the two scenes. Is John Grady a romantic who always feels his life is over after a romance has ended? Is this just a youthful reaction? Would Rawlins feel this way in a similar situation?

(7) What does this novel teach the reader about horses?

(8) What is the significance of the chess-playing scene between Alejandra's great-aunt and John Grady?

(9) How would you characterize Blevins? Why do John Grady and Rawlins disagree about Blevins and what to do with him?

(10) What is the significance of the scene early in the novel when they take down a fence, lead their horses over it, and then carefully put it back in place?

(11) When the wax traders try to buy Blevins, why is John Grady so appalled? How does this highlight his American sense of justice and equality that gets him into so much trouble with the great-aunt and other Mexican authorities?

(12) What are the differences between American and Mexican values? Illustrate with specific scenes from the novel.

(13) In addition to the horses, what are the elements of commonality between John Grady and his Mexican friends?

(14) What is the most horrific event in the novel?

(15) Why does John Grady become a wanderer and outcast?

(16) Why does Rawlins go back to his family?

(17) Why did Blevins pick the Jimmy Blevins name, after a radio preacher?

(18) Write about the influence of a great author (Faulkner, Cervantes, Dostoevsky, Camus, Twain, or London, for example) on McCarthy's book.

(19) What are the various meanings of the journey as a theme in the novel?

(20) What role do the good Samaritans John Grady meets along his journey play in the novel?

(21) What, if any, religious significance is present in the last scene of the book?

SELECTED BIBLIOGRAPHY

MCCARTHY'S MAJOR WORKS

Novels

The Orchard Keeper. 1965. New York: Vintage Books, 1993.

Outer Dark. 1968. New York: Vintage Books, 1993.

Child of God. 1974. New York: Vintage Books, 1993.

Suttree. 1979. New York: Vintage Books, 1992.

Blood Meridian, Or, the Evening Redness in the West. 1985. New York: Vintage Books, 1992.

All the Pretty Horses. 1992. New York: Vintage Books, 1993.

The Crossing. 1994. New York: Vintage Books, 1995.

Cities of the Plain. 1998. New York: Vintage Books, 1999.

Plays

The Stonemason: A Play in Five Acts. 1994. New York: Vintage Books, 1995.

Screenplays

The Gardener's Son. 1996. New York: Ecco Press, 1996.

CRITICAL WORKS ABOUT MCCARTHY AND THE SOUTHWEST

ARNOLD, EDWIN T. AND DIANNE C. LUCE. *Perspectives on Cormac McCarthy.* Jackson: University Press of Mississippi, 1999.

BUDIANSKY, STEPHEN. "Exploring Equine Evolution, Intelligence, and Behavior." *The Nature of Horses.* New York: The Free Press, 1997.

COGGINS, JACK. *The Horseman's Bible,* rev. ed. New York: Doubleday, 1984.

EDWARDS, ELWYN HARTLEY. *Horses.* New York: DK Publishing, 1993.

Emerging Literature of the Southwest Culture. El Paso: The University of Texas at El Paso, 1997.

KIDD, JANE. *International Encyclopedia of Horse Breeds.* Tucson: HPBooks, Inc., 1986.

MCGUANE, THOMAS. *Some Horses.* New York: The Lyons Press, 1999.

PAVORD, TONY AND ROD FISHER. *The Equine Veterinary Manual.* New York: Howell Book House Inc., 1987.

PRINCE, ELEANOR AND GAYDELL M. COLLIER. *Basic Training for Horses, English and Western.* New York: Doubleday, 1989.

ROBERTS, MONTY. *The Man Who Listens to Horses.* New York: Ballantine Books, 1997.

SERPA, LOUISE L. AND LARRY MCMURTRY. *Rodeo.* New York: Aperture.

VAVRA, ROBERT. *Such is the Real Nature of Horses.* New York: William Morrow, 1979.

WATSON, LARRY. *Montana 1948.* Minneapolis: Milkweed Editions, 1993.

The author wishes to acknowledge the help of these people, whose expertise was invaluable:
Nebraska Cowboys: John Jochem, Glen Jochem, Andy Mentink, Mike Stachura, and Eric Lindsley.

NOTES

NOTES

NOTES

NOTES

NOTES